Critical
Connections

CRITICAL CONNECTIONS

The Step-by-Step Guide to Transform Your Business Through Referral Marketing

Evan Leepson, MBA

PMP
Paramount Market Publishing, Inc.

Paramount Market Publishing, Inc.

950 Danby Road, Suite 136

Ithaca, NY 14850

www.paramountbooks.com

Voice: 607-275-8100; 888-787-8100   Fax: 607-275-8101

Publisher: James Madden

Editorial Director: Doris Walsh

ISBN-10: 1-941688-36-5 | ISBN-13: 978-1-941688-36-6

To contact the author:

Leepson Consulting

evan@leepsonassociates.com

www.leepsonassociates.com

301-525-1557

To: *Allie, Max, Gail and Marc*

Contents

Introduction:
In the Beginning . . .

Critical Connections delivers answers to your burning marketing questions. Where do I begin? How do I deal with the anxiety coming from creating and implementing a marketing plan? What do I really need to know about social media? How do I get the best bang for my marketing buck?

Loaded with tips, tactics, quizzes, real-life stories and examples, this book will help you create your own customized marketing plan. It is part workbook and part self-help and resource guide, wrapped into one book written to involve you in every step of building your marketing plan. The strategies and tactics presented here are particularly helpful if you depend on referrals to build your business.

Why *Critical Connections* is Unique

Critical Connections addresses psychological blocks that can prevent you from being successful. Overcoming psychological blocks will allow you to create new paths to achieve your business goals. The workbook lays out step-by-step tactics geared to building business relationships using traditional and social media marketing tactics.

I wrote this book for people like you, small business owners, the self-employed, as well as those providing professional and personal services. It reframes the definition of marketing as the care and feeding of strategic relationships and presents an innovative framework for building and maintaining relationships. Compared with other books using traditional transactional models, this one focuses on the importance of relationships and personal interactions.

If you want to transform your business, are considering starting a second career, or a retirement business, *Critical Connections* is for you. This unique guide is based on strategies and tactics presented in my already popular marketing workshops.

Practical, helpful, action-oriented and *powerful* are some of the words past attendees used to describe my *Build an Action Plan to Transform Your Business* workshops. The same energy, creativity, and practicality are expressed in *Critical Connections,* the book version of the workshop.

Why Now?

Marketing books published before 2003 are outdated. Prior to 2003 there were no social media platforms and web and email were the only electronic means of marketing. LinkedIn launched in 2003, Facebook in 2004, and Twitter in 2006. The first smartphone was introduced in 2007. No other book on the market emphasizes the psychological and self-help approach to building and maintaining a marketing campaign. No other book presents a unique method to pressure test the impact of marketing strategies.

How It All Started

He stood before me, with his requisite corporate attire – dark suit, crisp white shirt, red tie, and an impressive title: VP of Marketing. I immediately tensed up when I saw him. I had no idea what to expect. I was working at a New York City medical center as its industrial liaison; the medical center was hesitant about using the job title of marketing manager. My manager and I were summoned to meet the new VP of Marketing (I guess it was okay to use the word marketing in his title) to discuss plans for promoting the new outpatient substance abuse treatment center. I was told this guy left his job at a multi-national corporation to take this position. Should I be impressed? What did he know about healthcare marketing? After all, I was the marketing guy.

"Have you ever written a marketing plan?"

"No."

"What qualifies you to do this?" he asked. I stopped breathing and felt myself slowly sink into the floor. I can't recall exactly what I blurted out in response to his question. Whatever I said, it wasn't good. It wasn't what he wanted to hear. I froze while he lectured me about the fact I didn't have a marketing background and I've never really done marketing.

I thought I did marketing. I worked with the sales team at a firm that managed corporate employee assistance programs. I promoted workshops and seminars at a mental health training institute. Okay, I did not have a degree in marketing. I had a Master's degree in social work. I thought I was doing marketing.

I was trying very hard to listen to what he was saying, but all I could think about was how inadequate I felt and how unprepared I was to answer his questions. Mr. VP handed me a ten-page document and said, "Here's an example of a marketing plan. Use it as a guide and write me a plan for your department."

In terms of the details of the meeting, all I remember was how humiliated I felt. I do remember that on the way back to my office, my manager tried to reassure me everything was going to turn out okay. I didn't feel reassured. Over the next few weeks, I gradually stopped feeling sorry for myself, got up, and did something. I read as much as I could about healthcare marketing (there was no internet then); I talked to healthcare marketing people; I took a marketing course. Several months later, I enrolled in an MBA program. I was on a roll, feeling good, confidence level high. At the medical center, I had some minor marketing successes.

With the help of the clinical staff, I organized a seminar for referring physicians. I met with individual corporate employee assistance program directors. My goal was to promote the substance abuse program as a viable treatment alternative for their employees. At a local healthcare conference, I headed up a team that staffed a booth in the exhibit hall. Because of these and other marketing activities, the number of referrals to the substance abuse program increased. Looking back, I was pleased with the results.

The story does not end here.

Fast-forward three years. I got a new job at a management consulting firm developing marketing plans for healthcare providers. The first plan I wrote was for an outpatient diagnostic imaging center. With the assistance of the center's staff,

I tried to implement the plan but hit a brick wall. None of the goals, objectives, strategies, and tactics I wanted to use made any sense to me in this situation.

Most of what I had read and learned about marketing was based on creating strategies aimed at promoting products, not services. For example, one key component of marketing is to create pricing strategies. In healthcare, consumers and providers have little or no control over pricing medical services. Payments to healthcare providers are based on what insurance companies and other third party payers (Medicare, Medicaid) will reimburse. I naively thought I could use the same marketing strategies to promote healthcare services. In fact, there was no way these marketing plans could work. Was the model flawed or was I? Marketing strategies that worked for corporate America did not work for healthcare.

I tore up the plan and collected my thoughts. With the help of the staff, I suggested that we implement just two straightforward tactics to promote the new center. The first tactic was to create a guide for referring physicians. The guide would include, among other information, an overview of the center's diagnostic imaging capabilities and instructions for patient examination preparation. The second tactic was to expand the administrator's responsibility to include liaison activities with the hospital staff. This was a good start for them.

A few months later, I met with another hospital administrator about the idea of creating a marketing plan for a new ambulatory healthcare center. The administrator told me about all the different relationships he would have to develop and sustain in order for the center to operate. Then it hit me. It's not about catchy billboards, compelling logos, or slick brochures. He needed a systematic way to develop and maintain relationships with referring physicians, hospital department managers, surrounding hospitals and their administrators, the public, civic associations, and on and on. Relationships were the key to marketing healthcare services. Eureka!

Right after my eureka experience, I realized the two tactics I created for the outpatient diagnostic imaging center were all about building and maintaining relationships with those in a position to refer patients.

The rest is history. I've been using my relationship-based marketing model with overwhelming success for the past 20 years. I've written articles and have given talks at medical and healthcare conferences. Now, I firmly believe marketing, for any type of business, is the art and science of managing strategic relationships.

A Book Full of Chapters

In my quest to build a strategic relationship with you, my reader, I'll be asking you to think about marketing in a new way, and challenge yourself to answer tough questions. I will urge you to build a creative and effective marketing plan to transform your business.

In **Chapter 1**, *The Marketer's Dilemma,* you'll follow Nicole's futile attempts at figuring out how to build her business. I'm sure you'll identify with some or all of Nicole's struggles. I'll present an innovative approach to marketing that focuses on managing strategic relationships. A unique feature of *Critical Connections* is the emphasis on having you look at your own psychological blocks that prevent you from being successful at marketing.

Chapter 2, *Write It Down and Say It Out Loud,* starts with creating a vision of your business. I'll challenge you to examine your personal psychological issues preventing you from being successful at marketing. You'll go through an exercise to generate practical ways to overcome these challenges.

Chapter 3, *Face Your Fears,* addresses two fears preventing you from becoming successful at marketing: fear of selling and fear of setting and discussing fees. You'll be asked a series of questions aimed at confronting your negative internal forces and then be challenged to "try something new." You'll learn the three most common blocks to marketing success.

Chapter 4, *Networking for Introverts,* is a guide for those of you who are shy. You'll learn how to survive and possibly thrive when attending a networking event. You'll be asked to take the Are You an Introvert quiz and develop your personalized Networking Plan of Action. Also, you'll discover six networking strategies applicable to both introverts and extroverts.

What Do You Say In and Out of an Elevator? is the title of **Chapter 5.** You'll learn two different types of sales or communication pitches: the Elevator Speech for referrers and the Power Message for customers. You'll have the opportunity to craft both speeches.

Chapter 6, *Know Your Customer,* delves into the world of how to understand your customers. We will have an in-depth discussion of critical quality factors using a technique called "Voice of Customer" methodology. You'll identify customers' wants and needs as they pertain to the product or service you provide.

Chapter 7, *Talk is Not Cheap,* reveals secret weapons used to enhance your communication and sales skills. You'll learn how to counter objections in sales situations. We'll discuss the art of listening using my three secret weapons. There is a special section called "How to Ask a Good Question (or two)." Many new business owners fail to communicate effectively when talking to potential customers and referral sources. One failure is using jargon. We'll discuss the pros and cons of using jargon and learn how to turn jargon into common words. You'll also be introduced to the Jargon Police.

In **Chapter 8,** *Managing Strategic Relationships,* you'll learn about this new definition of marketing as an organized plan for the care and feeding of strategic relationships. The chapter goes into detail and discusses the role of referral sources in building a business. You are asked to identify referral sources who are in a position to refer customers or clients and identify primary and secondary consumer markets using the "management of strategic relationships" model.

We'll discuss how, why and when to use traditional marketing and promotional strategies in **Chapter 9,** *Tools of the Trade 1: Traditional Methods.* You'll learn how to avoid making two damaging marketing mistakes. Then, you will take a deep dive and explore the world of traditional marketing, advertising, and promotional tactics: print, written, broadcast, and in-person methods. A comprehensive list of these tactics is presented.

Chapter 10 is *Tools of the Trade 2: Electronic Marketing Platforms.* This chapter is prefaced with a caveat: the internet is changing daily. Online marketing strategies which work today, might not work tomorrow. A three-step process to create an online or social media presence is presented. The features and benefits of electronic and social media vehicles are described. Social media and social networking (and branding) are discussed in terms of how to build business relationships rather than how to connect with friends and family. You'll enjoy taking the *Are You a Social Media Luddite?* quiz.

You'll follow the marketing adventures of three entrepreneurs in **Chapter 11,** *A Tale of Two Clothiers.*

In **Chapter 12,** *Tactical to Practical,* you'll read the advice of some experts.

Chapter 13, *Putting It All Together,* takes you through the final steps. The pieces of the marketing plan created throughout the book are now ready for you to synthesize. Strategic relationships are paired with tactics aimed at capturing business. We'll be using an innovative technique to determine how to get the best bang for your marketing buck.

And finally, **Chapter 14,** *It's A Wrap,* summarizes the key messages in *Critical Connections.*

CHAPTER 1

The Marketer's Dilemma

If you don't know where you're going, you'll end up someplace else.

—Yogi Berra

Where Do I Begin My Marketing Efforts?

I had the pleasure of meeting Nicole M. at my marketing strategy workshop. She was outgoing and very serious about making the most of the workshop. During the lunch break, Nicole told me her story. She taught high school math, algebra, and calculus for ten years before she left to raise her children. She recently graduated to the status of empty nester. Now the kids were attending college and she wanted to pursue her passion of helping high school students as a math tutor.

Nicole lives in an affluent suburb of Washington, D.C. She thought this area would be an ideal place to set up her tutoring services. She had some contacts in math departments at two local high schools. As she was to find out later, none of her contacts were still teaching at their respective high schools.

At the marketing workshop, I asked attendees why they were there. Nicole, like most of the others, said she did not know where to begin her marketing efforts. Other workshop attendees, who had established businesses, were interested in revitalizing their marketing efforts. Where do I begin my marketing efforts is the most common question I get from those starting or expanding a small business. At the start of the workshop, attendees also asked, "Do I need a brochure? How do I set up my website? What should my Yellow Pages advertisement look like?" These questions came as no surprise.

Planning is Like Re-arranging the Deck Chairs on the Titanic

Nicole told me about her foray into the world of marketing. It's not a pretty picture. When she first had the idea of starting her tutoring business, she talked to her brother-in-law and asked him what to do. He has an MBA and works as a marketing manager for a telecommunications firm. He told Nicole she needed a business plan. Nicole didn't speak the language of business or marketing. She didn't know what a business plan entailed. So, Nicole did what everyone else did. She went online and searched for "how to write a business plan." Browsing through the myriad of business plan outlines, templates, tips and advice, gave Nicole a big headache.

She couldn't figure out why writing a business plan would help her build a tutoring service. It didn't work for Nicole. But she was determined to find something useful online. She went back to the internet and searched for the words "marketing plans." Again, there were tons of resources at her fingertips. Nicole found this definition of marketing plans from Entrepreneur.com:

> A marketing plan is a written document that describes your advertising and marketing efforts for the coming year; it includes a statement of the marketing situation, a discussion of target markets and company positioning and a description of the marketing mix you intend to use to reach your marketing goals.

Nicole found that sample marketing plan outlines were geared for small businesses selling products, not services.

Selling products entails a completely different strategic approach to marketing. For example, if you are building a marketing plan to sell gardening supplies or cosmetics, your marketing and sales tactics are straightforward transactions. When you sell a product such as a garden hose, your customer shops for price and options: length, thickness, type of material, etc. There is little or no emotional involvement in the sale. The sale is transactional.

However, if you provide personal or professional services such as financial planning, tutoring, or any type of management consulting, your marketing and sales tactics are consultative, not transactional. Consultative selling requires you to build a relationship with potential clients or customers. Consultative selling is value driven not price driven. You must convince potential clients or customers that they are receiving a high quality service delivered by a knowledgeable provider. If you want to create an online store, you'll have to keep in mind that relationships with prospective and existing customers require a combination of effective sales tactics and relational strategies.

Nicole was skeptical that writing a marketing plan would help get her marketing activities up and running. "This is not what I need to be doing right now," Nicole said.

⇄

In this book, you'll build a marketing plan. You won't be using the traditional model presented above, but you'll use an innovative approach geared to your specific business needs.

You Get What You Pay For

Moving forward, Nicole's best friend suggested Nicole attend a two-hour seminar called *How to Use Facebook, YouTube, and Twitter to Build Your Business.* Some of the topics were: *Building Your Brand, Growing Your Audience, and How To Manage Your Online Reputation.* Nicole questioned how much information could be crowded into two hours. She wondered if she would have to spend her day Tweeting, posting on Facebook, blogging, or making YouTube videos in order to promote her tutoring service. "This is not for me. I'm not going to the seminar," she told her friend.

Some Temporary Relief

Nicole was apprehensive about the idea of using social media to promote her business. Her experience using social media was limited keeping up-to-date with the activities of her friends, former work colleagues, and family on Facebook. Fortunately, her two college-age sons introduced her to LinkedIn and Facebook's business pages. She now had a rudimentary understanding of what these platforms do. This temporarily relieved her anxiety.

Gigantic Numbers

> *Human beings cannot comprehend very large or very small numbers.*
> *It would be useful for us to acknowledge that fact.*   —Daniel Kahneman

While Nicole was searching online for help in starting her business, she came across The Pew Internet Research Project (www.pewinternet.org) and was struck by the amount of data they collected about social networking and online usage.

For example, according to Pew, 71 percent of online adults use Facebook, 17 percent use Instagram, 21 percent use Pinterest, and 22 percent use LinkedIn. She found Facebook alone has about 133 million users in the United States (www.internetworldstats.com/stats26.htm).

Nicole then went looking for potential tutoring referral sources near where she lived. She found 22 public high schools and 24 private high schools in her county. She found 64,200 students enrolled in public high schools and 5,300 enrolled in private high schools in her county. Nicole asked herself what could she do with these numbers. What do they mean? Am I going down another dead end? Reading all of this caused her to slip into a state of marketing paralysis.

It's been my experience that using gigantic numbers to convince customers or clients to purchase your product or service is cold and impersonal. For example, if I were promoting a diabetes-related product or service and wanted to use gigantic numbers to persuade potential customers to buy my product or service, I might say in my promotional literature and on my website: "29 million people in the USA have diabetes." You would probably say, "So what? How does that affect me?" Can you relate to 29 million of anything? But, if I asked, "Do you have a friend or family member who has diabetes?" most likely, you would say yes. This simple phrase might be an effective way to connect with your customers or clients.

Applying gigantic numbers (demographic or economic) to help you understand your market might not portray an accurate picture of your local target market. I am not referring to those of you who are considering opening an online store or providing an online service to a broad range of customers.

When I read statistics like those mentioned above, even I feel bowled over. Yes, most of the statistics are broken down by age, sex, or other variables. It doesn't help. But, the question for me is so what? How does any of this apply to me?

Boiling the Ocean

Nicole was stuck. There were too many marketing tools and techniques at her disposal to use to start promoting her tutoring services. Again, back to the beginning: "Where do I start?" When new clients come to me for help with their business, I ask what they have done and what they are planning to do to start promoting their business? I'll usually hear something like: "I'm working on my website. I just started Tweeting. I'm blogging. I'm planning to speak at an upcoming local seminar."

When I hear the litany of activities, I wonder if this person is trying to boil the ocean. The term "boil the ocean" is one of many business jargon phrases used to embellish a point. Boil the ocean means to take on too much, to over-extend yourself, or to be overly ambitious. This is a recipe for failure. Next time you are at the seashore (if you live inland, a large lake or river will do), try to take that entire body of water and boil it. How are you going to do it?

Now that you are disappointed you couldn't boil the ocean, try this. Take a teaspoon from your kitchen drawer. Go back to the ocean, river, or lake you just visited. Dip the teaspoon in the ocean. Use a lighter and place it under the teaspoon and see what happens. In a matter of minutes, the water will boil. Congratulations, you have successfully boiled a teaspoon of ocean. So, what's the point here? Be realistic in how much you can do. I assume everyone has just so much time, money, and energy to devote to building a business. How many marketing related projects can anyone take on at a time? Next time think teaspoon.

Do I Really Need a Branding Iron?

Nicole's next dead end centered around the need to start branding herself. She heard friends say, "You have to brand yourself. You have to have a logo and you must have a website. After all, how are people going to find you? How are you going to stand out from your competition?"

Nicole thought about what a brand is. She visualized McDonald's golden arches. Then she pictured the CNN logo. What's this logo stuff all about? She learned, from looking online that the McDonald's arches are called icons or symbols and CNN is text-only type called a "word mark." Some businesses have both. An example of a combination logo is FedEx. If you look carefully at FedEx's logo, you'll see a white arrow between the E and the X pointing to the right.

Is this where I start? Do I need a logo, mark, or a combination? How do I find someone to do this? How much is a logo design going to cost me? Do I look online? Do I go to an advertising or marketing communications agency? What about using a graphic design firm? Or hire a freelancer? Why do I need it now? Too many questions; too few answers. Her headache intensified.

How Not to Get Stuck

A coaching client of mine, James, was making progress building his financial planning service. He met with referral sources, got listed on a web-based directory of financial planners, and gave several talks at civic and business seminars. His referral stream began to flow. James did all the right things to start his financial planning business. After four months James decided he needed a logo and a website. He had no idea where to start. He had few contacts outside the financial planning community who could help him find a logo designer or website developer.

We agreed to move forward with hiring a logo and web designer. I would contact four web builders who also create logos. I would screen them and present James with my recommendations. After screening four designers, the choice came down to two graphic design studios. James selected one studio. I took on the role of assisting him through the process from concept to implementation.

Moral to the story: start creating and implementing effective marketing strategies before delving into the world of logos and websites. Once you're up and running, you might find your business is moving in a direction you did not expect. You do not want to get stuck with a logo or website which does not accurately represent your business.

Initially, James did not have a logo or personal website. However, he did have an online presence by getting listed on a financial planner referral list. When someone searches for your name or business and can't find you, say goodbye to your business. This is especially true for those who want to promote a personal or professional service.

A Light at the End of the Tunnel

Back to Nicole's marketing journey. Nicole's husband, Nick, suggested she look at the Small Business Administration's (SBA) website. He said there is information there about how to apply for an SBA loan. So, Nicole went to the SBA's website and tried to wade through the topics to find what she needed. There were all sorts of resources available on how to start and manage a small business. For example, you can find information on how to forecast growth, how to build a franchise, what to know about business law and regulations. You can take as many as 42 online small business training courses. There are 69 videos to watch. Nicole was about to give up on the SBA website when she stumbled upon a tab called Local Assistance. She found her local Economic Development Council and immediately contacted them. The Economic Development Council's business advisor suggested she attend my marketing workshop.

After Nicole attended my marketing seminar, she was able to focus and felt confident about where to start. After the workshop, Nicole periodically kept in touch and updated me on her progress.

Overcoming Marketing Paralysis

Marketing paralysis is a syndrome commonly seen in people like Nicole who are experts in their field but have little knowledge and experience in marketing. Marketing paralysis is also found in those who have a good idea for a business but do not know how to take the idea out of their head and do something with it.

Marketing paralysis is different from analysis paralysis. Analysis paralysis is over-analyzing a situation or idea to the point that nothing ever gets done. Those individuals or groups suffering from analysis paralysis usually say something like, "We need more data. Let's start from the beginning again. We need to get the right people to work on this." Consequently, the project stagnates and in many cases, no decisions are made.

There are recognizable signs and indicators of marketing paralysis. You don't have to exhibit all three signs and symptoms to suffer from marketing paralysis. Nicole exhibited three of the most common signs and symptoms.

1. **The glaze.** She had a glazed-over look in her eyes when anyone mentioned the dreaded word "marketing."

2. **Narrow thinking.** Her thinking got narrower and narrower. She had an irresistible urge to wallow in the weeds of her situation. Rather than taking a step back and looking at the bigger picture, she focused on minute details: colors for her website, finding key words to be used in her website, ruminating about which social media platform to use, etc.

3. **Second guessing.** Nicole would second guess herself and question any decision she made. The result was a total shut down of her marketing efforts. Not good.

If you suffer the pain and agony of marketing paralysis, don't worry. Help is on the way. You can get immediate as well as long-term relief from marketing paralysis by applying the following tips to your unique situation.

Overcoming Marketing Paralysis

Tip #1: Think global, act local

I've taken the liberty of adapting the concept of "think global, act local" to help you overcome marketing paralysis. Let's break this down: By thinking globally, you keep your eye on business trends. You can do this by subscribing to industry publications or attending national seminars and conferences in your field of expertise.

If you're planning to open an online retail store (virtual storefront) you should think global. Your customers are located all over the map. Generally speaking, there is no need to act locally. However, you might want to act locally and, for example, set up a pop-up shop in your home area. A pop-up shop is an alternative to the traditional retail store you would find in a mall. They are usually open for a few days to a few weeks and are found in areas of high foot traffic. The most important benefit pop-ups offer is the ability for you to make a personal connection with customers. The pop-up retail format allows you to personally get to know your customers and build stronger relationships.

Nicole looked online and found information about new video math games and the latest math tutoring theories. She scoured the national association of math tutors website for new math tutoring techniques. She looked globally so she could act locally.

Tip #2: Phone a friend

It's always a good idea to talk things over with a friend and get some advice. You might want to discuss a new idea, clarify a stumbling block, or just plain talk about your business. If you're considering starting a solo business, it gets lonely quickly in the early stages of planning your business strategies.

Phone a friend who is not employed in your industry or profession. You want fresh eyes on your situation. You want the other person's perspective.

When you initially talk with your friends, do not ask your friends to solve your problem for you. Do not let them give you advice. Ask them to listen and act as a sounding board. Sometimes, just saying aloud what your situation is can be helpful. Now, you can brainstorm ideas or solutions.

People love to give advice. When someone gives you advice, the advice is more about what the other person needs rather than what you need. Be aware.

Tip #3: Write it down

Get a piece of paper and in one or two sentences write down your answers to the following questions.

Question #1. *What is unique about the product or service I provide?*

_____

_____

_____

Question #2. *What am I passionate about?*

_____

_____

_____

Question #3. *How can I share my passion?*

_____

_____

_____

If, after ten minutes you are stuck and can't answer any of the questions, do the following:

- Take a break and step far away from your computer.
- Go for a walk.
- Do three push-ups or drink a cup of decaffeinated coffee.

Now go back and see what happens. Can you answer these questions to the best of your ability? Save this piece of paper and either tape it to your bathroom mirror or place it somewhere near your computer. If you have taken my advice, phoned a friend, and answered these tough questions, you are ready for Tip #4.

Tip #4: Do one thing every day that scares you.

This quote had been ascribed to Eleanor Roosevelt, but there is no clear indication she actually said it. However, the idea of doing something scary is often paralyzing, but compelling. Rather than worrying about your phone not ringing or your email inbox being empty, do one thing to move your business forward. Do one thing today and one thing tomorrow. After reading *Critical Connections*, you'll have a written game plan with plenty of things to do. Some of these things will scare you, and some won't.

At this point, you might have some ideas about how to build your business. List two scary activities you think will help move your business forward.

One scary thing I will do tomorrow _____

_____ .

One scary thing I will do the next day _____

_____ .

A New Way of Looking at Marketing

Here's your next assignment. Ask six friends, colleagues, family members, business school graduates, or small business owners to define the word "marketing." If possible ask them to define it in one paragraph or less. Most likely, you'll get six different answers or maybe even seven. I found a website listing 72 different definitions of marketing. When I looked at these definitions, all I could think of was poor Nicole, frozen in her tracks.

Before I present my definition of marketing (I hope mine can be added as #73 on the above list), here's what marketing isn't:

- Creating an advertising campaign
- Building a website
- Tweeting or blogging or posting on Facebook
- Using public relations
- Going to the grocery store

My definition:

Marketing is the management of strategic relationships.

As I mentioned earlier, most definitions shy away from the aspect of relationships. My model is relational not transactional. It focuses on building and maintaining business relationships rather than primarily concentrating on making the sale. Marketing is about delivering products and services, which meet your customers' needs. Another way to think about this definition is to say that marketing is all about creating a caring and feeding program for strategic relationships.

If you want to start a web-based business, don't fool yourself into thinking that all you have to do is build a website, post on Facebook, Tweet or blog. You have to build, sustain, and take care of all business relationships.

There are two types of strategic relationships: one strategic relationship is with potential and existing customers or clients. The second strategic relationship is with those individuals who are in a position to refer customers or clients (referral sources). In the next chapter, we'll take a deep dive into the world of strategic relationships.

In the rush to use exciting new online technology, one key factor is left out – the customer. What about the customer?

Business-to-Business (B2B) and Business-to-Consumer (B2C): What's the big deal?

There is a great deal written about the difference between B2B and B2C marketing. In a nutshell, B2B transactions and marketing strategies occur between businesses. Think of a manufacturer selling its product to a wholesaler or a wholesaler selling to a retail outlet. B2C transactions and marketing strategies are directly between a company and its consumers.

Whether your customer is a business or an individual, the same thing holds true: Your job is to build and manage strategic relationships. And, that's what *Critical Connections* is all about.

CHAPTER 2

Write It Down and Say It Out Loud

Vision without action is merely a dream. Action without vision just passes the time. Vision with action can change the world.

—Joel A. Barker

A unique feature of *Critical Connections* is the emphasis on asking you to look inside yourself. Don't panic or close the book. I won't be leading you down some touchy-feely path or spewing self-help clichés and platitudes. In this fun chapter, you'll create a vision of what you want your business to be. You'll look into the psychological blocks preventing you from being successful at marketing. Exercises are presented to help you both understand and overcome your stumbling blocks and doubts about your ability to be a successful marketer.

Have you ever met an entrepreneur who has a great idea for a business and wants desperately to tell you about it? Did you feel the entrepreneur's sense of excitement and passion? Did the entrepreneur paint a colorful picture of his or her idea? Did you get swept up in the moment? Did you find yourself telling others about what this entrepreneur said?

Creating Your Vision

The dictionary defines a vision as the act or power of anticipating what will or may come to be. Your goal is not to predict the future, but to set your eyes on the prize. You can create and recreate your vision at any time, from the embryonic stage to being up and running.

Let's see what Deepak Chopra has to say in his book *The Spontaneous Fulfillment of Desire: Harnessing the Infinite Power of Coincidence to Create Miracles*:

Consciousness orchestrates its activity in response to both attention and intention. Whatever you put your attention on becomes energized. Whatever you take your attention away from dwindles. On the other hand, intention is the key to transformation, as we have seen. So, you could say that attention activates the energy field, and intention activates the information field, which causes transformation.

Deepak believes energy follows attention. In other words, what you focus on can become your reality. If you put your vision out there into the universe (it might be a bit extreme, but it does make a point), you'll have a good chance of making your vision happen. If you set your intention to work toward your vision, your chances of success increase.

Your vision:

- Is intangible.
- Is intentional.
- Serves as a motivational force.
- Expresses your passion.
- Is a guide for planning your business objectives.

Let's go deeper.

- Your vision, when written, serves as a constant reminder of where you're going.
- Your vision should be action-oriented.
- It should be worded in such a way as there is room for change.
- You should always keep your potential customer or client in the front of your mind when creating a vision. After all, isn't your business about providing a product or service that will satisfy a customer or client need?
- The elegant aspect of a vision is that while you are crafting it, you are painting a mental picture based on your emotions (passion) and your intellect (your business idea).
- The result is a written statement about your dream for your business.

Can you keep your ambitious goal in mind and at the same time focus on concrete, tangible outcomes? I believe this is the key to success. You set a path and follow it. The path might be bumpy, with dangerous curves, hills, and dead ends, but in the end, you'll get what you want – a successful business based on your values and your unique skills and abilities. It's easy to get sidetracked and lose sight of your vision. There are many tempting distractions out there.

Your vision is not about the path, it's about where the path takes you. It's all about finding your passion and pursuing it. In times of doubt, you can revisit your goal, and hopefully feel encouraged.

Backward Visioning

Here's the problem most people have when asked, "What's your vision for your business?" They usually stumble and have a hard time painting a clear picture of the future, because it's almost impossible to think of what might happen in the future. It's hard to predict where you will wind up. If predicting a vision isn't an effective method, what is the best way to define and articulate your vision?

I find that if you look backwards and describe what you've accomplished, you'll be able to imagine your vision. Your accomplishments are concrete manifestations of your vision. When you can describe your accomplishments, you'll know you're on your way to fulfilling your vision. However, it is easier to say where you have been, which leads to the idea of backwards visioning. The technique of backwards visioning is an effective tool to help you create your vision.

Before we peer into the world of visioning, let's see how others created their vision.

Here's an example of how someone lost his vision and found it again, changing his life. In college, Mitchell was passionate about tackling climate change issues. Mitchell's passion was put on hold during his last year of college when he focused his energy on getting accepted to law school. In law school, he focused on getting good grades. He focused on getting a good internship in order to land a good job.

After graduating from law school, Mitchell landed a great job as an attorney in the tax practice of a midsized law firm. He worked hard to make a name for himself and become a trusted associate. However, it took a toll on him. He had to work long hours and had little free time on the weekends to pursue outside activities. His social life disappeared. Eventually, Mitchell dreaded coming to work. He felt exhausted all the time. He did not feel motivated. He hoped no one in the law firm would notice how rundown he was.

⇆

Mitchell lost sight of his passion when he landed the job as tax attorney.

Mitchell wanted out of the law firm. He kept on saying to himself, practicing law is not for me. He told himself he wasn't cut out for being a lawyer. He needed a new career.

From a career development perspective, we want to know if Mitchell was dissatisfied with his current working environment or dissatisfied with his career choice? These are two very different issues. The symptoms might be the same, but the problem is different. For example, if you dislike your boss or complain about not being challenged, you might think you need to change careers. But at a deeper level, all you might need is a change of scenery – working a similar type of job with a new employer in your industry. Or, working the same type of job in another industry.

Mitchell was convinced he needed a new career so he could jump-start his life. One day, Mitchell was talking to his college friend, Rebecca. She and Mitchell were active in campus organizations that focused on environmental issues. He was impressed with how energetic and enthusiastic she was at her job at Environment America. Mitchell was surprised by his own excitement when listening to Rebecca. He remembered how fulfilled he felt in college working on these issues.

Upon further examination, Mitchell realized he valued his ability to help people with legal problems. He knew he could combine his legal expertise with his passion to contribute to a greener planet. This was a clear case of "everything Mitchell needed was right in front of him." All he had to do was look inside.

He began to create a vision of what his professional life would be like in five years. And using the backwards visioning technique, Mitchell was able to set his agenda.

VISIONING EXERCISE

Here is the scenario. Imagine it is five years in the future. You are attending a conference, seminar, or some kind of networking event. You bump into an old friend you haven't seen in years. What a nice surprise! This friend does not know

Your vision can be expressed in terms of what you have accomplished on your way to fulfilling your vision.

that you started your own business. You're excited and can't wait to tell this person about what you've professionally accomplished since you started your own business.

In order to complete this exercise, you should keep the following two thoughts in mind.

1. You are writing this as if you are in the future. Since you are in the future, you'll be looking back at what you accomplished; you'll be writing your thoughts in the past tense, not in the future tense.

2. When you say your vision out loud, you say it in the past tense. *This is easier said than done.* By saying out loud and writing down your accomplishments, you're telling the world (or at least your friend) you have achieved certain milestones that are part of your vision.

Here's an example of someone who dreamed big and used backwards visioning to set her direction. Tracy is a 35-year-old social worker with a Master's Degree. Recently, she left her job as a clinical social worker at a social service agency. She specialized in marriage and family counseling and is certified as a marriage and family therapist. Her goal was to create a private practice. Here's what she wrote:

My practice is flourishing and it employs three therapists who see clients mostly during the day. We are available at the practice 7 days a week from 7am - 9pm. We see very few clients in the evenings so we can spend more time with our families. We conduct four premarital educational seminars a year. We are bringing in enough revenue to buy technology (i.e. computers and data storage) to support our work. We conducted a staff retreat at a beach location. The community has become enriched and strengthened from the counseling services we provide. We are involved in community projects and donate our time for different causes.

So, let's begin.

⇄ BACKWARDS VISIONING EXERCISE #1
Answer the Tough Questions

Call it a vision or a dream; you'll want to ask yourself some hard questions before you attempt to write it. Take a piece of paper from a pad or notebook.

When you're answering these questions, aim for a directionally correct vision. You're not looking for perfection. Directionally correct means you're going in the general direction. This exercise is a not a test. You will not be graded. You will not be penalized for misspelling or grammar.

Answer the following tough questions.

1. What is my highest dream or vision for my business?

2. What do I wish for the most?

3. What can I put into words that I have never put into words before?

4. What am I willing to do to make my vision come true?

5. What resources do I need to use on the way to achieving my vision?

⇆ BACKWARDS VISIONING EXERCISE #2
Dream Big

Take another piece of paper from a pad or notebook.

Take up to five minutes to think about and write your thoughts, ideas, feelings, or key words which describe your vision and the professional accomplishments that would help you attain your vision of your business. Write whatever comes to mind. Do not worry about spelling or grammar. It might be easy for you to write using bullet points to help condense your thoughts. You have time to edit this later. Don't censor yourself. Don't beat yourself up. You might want to use your senses: sight, smell, taste, feel, and touch to make your vision more meaningful and powerful to you. Think big; don't be afraid to go out of your comfort zone.

Think little goals and expect little achievements. Think big goals and win big success. —David Joseph Schwartz, *The Magic of Thinking Big*

Go back and using the information from Exercise 1, write it in the past tense. Remember, it's five years from today. You can start with the following:

It is the year 2020. I created my own _____

Write your vision here: _____

_____

_____

_____

_____

_____

_____

Walk away from your desk for at least five minutes. When you return, take time to tighten up what you wrote. Add, delete or modify as you wish.

Clean it up.

After you are happy with your vision, say it out loud to anyone who will listen. Be sure to preface your statement by telling the listener the year is 2020. If you say something that doesn't feel right, delete it or modify as needed.

Make a copy of your vision statement and prominently post it where it is easy for you to see. I've had some clients write their vision and laminate it in plastic and carry it with them. Others like to tape it to their desk.

Congratulations, you just created a working draft and blueprint for your future.

Everything you say and do to build your business should be in the service of fulfilling your vision.

Time to Get Personal

Here's where you have the opportunity to examine your strengths, which will help you reach your vision, and the challenges that might prevent you from becoming successful at marketing, which in turn might prevent you from moving toward your vision. Why are we exploring this? In my marketing workshops, when participants explore their strengths and confront their challenges, they feel better equipped to make their vision a reality. I think this section of *Critical Connections* is the most important section of the book. Why? If you clearly identify your strengths and challenges, you'll be able to build on your strengths to meet any challenge that might pop up along the way.

The discussion of strengths and challenges is the most important topic in this book. Your marketing efforts will surely stall out if your strengths and challenges are not addressed.

A strength is a trait, characteristic, or skill that comes effortlessly to you. Sometimes others recognize your strengths while you minimize them. We usually take our strengths for granted. If something comes naturally to you, it's a strength. Most likely you enjoy using your strengths. You've always valued your strengths. In a more ethereal sense, you can't be great at doing something unless it's a strength.

Did you notice I have not used the word weakness during my introductory comments about strengths and challenges? I equate weakness with helplessness. I see the word weakness as a fault emanating from the world of negativity. Not good. Living in a world of negativity is a bummer. Negativity begets itself.

A challenge is some activity that takes you out of your emotional and intellectual comfort zone and could cause anxiety. When you face a challenge, you'll need to harness many of your internal strengths to overcome the challenge. It's out of your comfort zone. My psychotherapist friends like to say that dealing with a challenge can be an area of personal growth.

There are two different approaches to working with your strengths and challenges. In the first approach, you identify your strengths and use them to their fullest advantage. In the second approach, you recognize your challenges and work to overcome them. Your strengths are not necessarily related to your challenges, but they can be.

Here's an example of how one of my marketing workshop participants worked on his strengths and challenges. Ben is a 28-year-old graphic designer. He currently works for an advertising agency and wants to leave the agency to start his own graphic design studio. I asked him to tell me one key strength he brings to marketing or building his business. He immediately replied, "I'm creative!"

Next, I asked Ben to describe the most difficult challenge he faces in marketing or in building his business. He hesitated for a few seconds, and then said, "I'm always second guessing myself about my ability to be creative. I question whether I'm able to sell and whether I'm good enough to compete in the market." For the first time ever, Ben was able to articulate his challenge.

Next question. I asked Ben to look carefully at his difficult challenge. Then I probed deeper and asked him if there is something more he might know about second guessing himself. Ben looked down for a few seconds. He seemed to be somewhere else in his mind. "I don't know."

Next question. "Ben, think hard now. What, if any internal messages do you have about yourself or marketing which would make it difficult for you to overcome your challenge?" Now Ben was deep in thought. "I'm not smart enough to be doing this," Ben revealed. "My parents always compared me to my older brother who I perceived as being smart. But it extends farther than that. I just had a memory flash. I'm in fifth grade and my teacher, Mrs. Peterson calls my mother in for an after school conference. Oh boy, I'm in trouble now. Mrs. Peterson told my mother I have no imagination! From that day on I thought I wasn't smart enough. Yikes. No wonder why I'm second guessing everything. I equated having no imagination with not being smart."

"Ben," I asked, "is there a positive message you would like to have for yourself to replace your negative message?" Ben replied, "I'm a competent, creative professional." I gave Ben a pen and an index card and asked him to:

1. Write this positive message on the card.

2. Display the card in a prominent place where you can see it every day.

Now that Ben had a clear picture of his positive message, we went on to the next part of the exercise. I asked Ben if he had at least one concrete idea to address his challenge of second guessing himself. Ben, feeling more confident, said he would make a list of his recent accomplishments.

Finally, I asked the other workshop participants if they had any ideas to help Ben.

Someone suggested that Ben call one of his colleagues and friends to remind him that he's a competent professional. Another suggested that Ben reread his list of accomplishments when he starts to second guess himself. My suggestion was a straightforward message for Ben to say to himself: "It's okay to make mistakes."

Ben was candid about his struggle with second guessing himself. He took a good, hard look at himself. After the workshop Ben told me he felt like a burden had been lifted off his back. Good work, Ben.

Now it's your turn.

⇆ WORKING WITH YOUR STRENGTHS AND CHALLENGES: EXERCISE #1

Use the space below to answer the following questions.

1. What are 3 or 4 key strengths you bring to marketing or building your business?

_____

_____

_____

_____

2. What are 3 or 4 challenges you face in marketing or building your business?

_____

_____

_____

_____

3. Looking at your most difficult challenge you wrote in #2, is there something more you know about this challenge?

_____

_____

_____

_____

4. Think hard now. What, if any internal messages do you have about yourself and marketing that would make it difficult for you to overcome your main challenge?

_____

_____

_____

_____

5. Is there a positive message you have about yourself that can replace your negative message?

_____

_____

_____

_____

6. List several ideas you have to deal with your main challenge:

_____

_____

_____

_____

_____

_____

_____

_____

_____

_____

After you have answered the above questions as best you can, discuss your responses with a friend. Ask your friend if he or she has any suggestions for you in response to Question #6.

_____

_____

_____

_____

In this chapter, you figured out where you're going with you business by creating a vision. You tackled some of the personal challenges you'll face. You identified your unique strengths, which you can capitalize on to create your vision. I encourage you to visit and revisit your vision. When you face a new challenge, go back and work the Strengths and Challenges Exercise.

CHAPTER 3

Face Your Fears

Two of the most frustrating challenges preventing you from becoming successful at marketing are a fear of selling and a fear of setting and discussing fees. Before we explore your fears, I'd like to discuss brain chemistry. What does the chemistry of your brain have to do with being a successful marketer? Plenty. Read on and you'll see what I'm talking about.

Have you ever noticed when you're in a conversation and the other person says something that irritates you, strikes a nerve in you, or insults you, you might have a visceral reaction? Your pulse quickens. Your thoughts start racing. You are on high alert. Some part of your brain senses some kind of danger, whether it is real or imagined. Some might call this response an over-reaction to the situation. Let's look at it from a neuroscience perspective.

Time out for a quick tutorial of how your brain functions in terms of processing fear and danger. This is not a discussion of how your brain works in general. The following information is taken from *Mindsight: The New Science of Personal Transformation* by Daniel J. Seigel (Bantam Books, 2010).

There are three parts of your brain: the brain stem, the limbic region, and the cortex.

The brain stem is the most primitive part of the brain, sometimes referred to as the brain stem or reptilian brain. This part of your brain keeps you alive. The reptilian brain controls basic bodily processes such as regulating the lungs and heart. It senses, acts, and tells us how to survive, eat, drink, and protect ourselves. We share these basic instincts with all animals. The brain stem instantly detects danger and is activated when, for example, you engage in the irritating conversation mentioned above.

The limbic region is a part of your brain with numerous structures. Susan Cain (we'll hear more from Susan in Chapter 4) said the following about the limbic region in *Quiet: The Power of Introverts in a World that Can't Stop Talking* (Broadway Books, 2012):

> Scientists dislike the phrase "limbic system." No one really knows what parts of the brain this refers to. Many use the term to mean brain areas that have something to do with emotion. Still, it's a useful shorthand.

The amygdala is a part of the limbic system involved in the activation of emotion. It plays a role in the appraisal of meaning and decoding social signals. It also sounds an alarm like a smoke detector when receiving data that suggests there may be a fire. However, the limbic system also includes the hippocampus, which has a primary role in memory, specifically the recall of facts and autobiographical details. The hippocampus regulates how perceptions are categorized and manages emotional appraisal.

The hippocampus, using its memory and perceptions helps decode the level of alert. For instance, did I burn the toast or is the kitchen really on fire? The limbic system as a whole integrates many mental processes by receiving information from the brain stem, body, and the higher cortical regions. So, while the amygdala sounds the alarm bell, the limbic system, particularly the hippocampus, actually does some evaluation of a threat.

However, the amygdala is strengthened by cortisol, the "stress hormone." The alarm bells tend to get louder, but cortisol tends to shrink the hippocampus. So, the very structure in the limbic system, which moderates the amygdala's demanding response, weakens in the face of stress.

Here Comes the Vicious Cycle of Stress

Your limbic region receives messages from your brain stem telling you danger is imminent, no matter how hazardous or innocuous the object of fear is. There is a reason for this. Fear often helps us with self-preservation. We perceive fear, as well as related emotions, in order to protect ourselves from danger and heighten our awareness. The limbic system has no ability to distinguish danger from an approaching mouse or from a rampaging elephant. It just senses danger. And, in fact, the limbic system is constantly scanning for danger. Seigel says: "When we are stressed, we secrete a hormone that stimulates the adrenals to release cortisol, which mobilizes energy by putting our entire metabolism on high alert to meet the challenge."

For our brief discussion, the third part of the brain called the cortex includes your pre-frontal cortex. The cortex is the thinking and action part of your brain. For our purposes, we will focus on the pre-frontal cortex, which is the part of your cortex located in the front of your brain. While there are many functions of the pre-frontal cortex, we will discuss just a few. The pre-frontal cortex allows you to ponder the nature of the universe (think about the future), evaluate situations, provide social control, and it regulates the limbic system and brain stem. It also soothes unwanted fears. In Seigel's words, the pre-frontal cortex "allows us to think about thinking."

In a recent study, researchers found that when people use self-talk (more about this later in this chapter) to reassess upsetting situations, activity in their pre-frontal cortex increases in an amount correlated with a decrease of activity in their amygdala. The activity was measured by using functional MRI, which is an imaging technology that measures brain activity by detecting associated changes in blood flow.

What Does this Have to Do with Marketing?

Here's a good example of what happens when your pre-frontal cortex shuts down in the so-called face of danger. A customer says to you the product you sold him was useless. Or, a customer chastises you for not delivering what you promised. You have many years of experience and are confident about the quality of your work. However, remembering your experience and confidence does not help you. You find yourself getting furious. What is happening here is your reptilian brain and limbic system are activated and your thinking and mental processes shut down. You regress to using your reptilian brain and limbic system and wind up in the land of reactivity. Not pleasant.

What happens when you find yourself in the land of reactivity? Let's hear Tamara's story. Tamara is a 29-year-old freelance destination-wedding planner. She left her job as a lowly administrative assistant at a large event planning company. During her time there she made solid contacts in the hospitality industry with hotel managers, airline personnel, photographers, videographers, florists, bridal consultants, disc jockeys, bands, etc. She felt confident she could make it on her own.

Tamara did not fully realize that she had to develop trusting business relationships with both her clients (the bride and groom and their respective parents) who are hiring her to plan the event and the vendors who would provide the services requested. She began to feel overwhelmed at the thought of dealing with all these people. She also got nervous thinking about working with overseas venues.

Tamara was fortunate and got a referral from a former colleague. This would be Tamara's first client. When Tamara's friend told her about the referral, Tamara's brain went into overdrive and she felt nervous, to say the least. She remained in this stirred up state right up until the time she met face-to-face with the prospective client.

Her nervousness led to what I call the "Look Out Syndrome." The Look Out Syndrome occurs when you are in a situation with another person and you focus your attention on the other person's body language, his or her facial expressions or general demeanor instead of listening to what is being said. Often, your evaluation of these non-verbal cues is incorrect and usually negative. When you have this syndrome, you usually imagine the other person is thinking negative thoughts about you. The Look Out Syndrome is one of many adaptations we use to scan for danger. Not only was Tamara scanning for danger by looking out, she also was questioning herself, "Will I get the sale?" Now more doubts about her confidence started creeping into her head. Tamara said to herself, "Is the look on the other person's face saying he doesn't want to work with me?" This is called negative self-talk. As a result she didn't hear most of what the prospective client wanted. Not good.

Here's another way to look at the Look Out Syndrome:

I am looking at you looking at me.

And

I am wondering what you're thinking about me.

What a mess. When you're taking on the role of Look Out and not listening, you don't say what you want to say because you're too busy trying to figure out what the other person is thinking. Can we attribute Tamara's case of Looking Out to inexperience? Immaturity? No self-control? Probably none of these.

Tamara was scanning the prospective client so intensely she asked the same question three times. Clearly, Tamara's thinking brain (pre-frontal cortex) was offline, and only her danger signals (her limbic system and reptilian brain) were online. The prospective client did not hire Tamara.

Tips to Get Your Brain Back Online and How to Overcome the Look Out Syndrome

1. **Look at the other person, not into them.** Focus on the color of their eyes, the color of their hair, or any other feature. Focusing on physical features will calm your brain so your thoughts stay focused in the present. Then there is no room to think what they're thinking about you.

2. **Listen.** This is probably the easiest thing in the world to say and the most difficult thing in the world to do. What is listening? How do you listen? How do you know if you're being listened to? Don't fret about these questions. You'll be learning some effective listening skills you can immediately use when you read Chapter 7.

3. **Turn that frown upside down.** I'm a big fan of faking it – to a point. Pretend to be brave when you're anxious. Try it and you might feel more self-assured. Fake being interested in other people when you're feeling low. See what happens to you.

4. **Become a member of the Welcome Wagon team.** As a textbook introvert, I quiver at the idea of attending a social event where I have to talk to strangers. Gail, my wife, sometimes tells me, "Evan, be welcoming instead of sitting in a corner and texting on your phone." If I take a deep breathe, I can begin to calm my nervous system. Then I realize that if I isolate myself, I'll feel more embarrassed. I tell myself to think of an easy topic and find someone to talk to. I usually enjoy myself and have calmed myself down.

5. **Take a timeout.** I used to watch television as a way to calm myself down. However, I found watching TV got me more stirred up. According to a 2013 study published in the *Journal of Communication*, ". . . people stressed from work did not feel any more relaxed after they played video games or watched television. They often felt even worse." In business situations, I generally remove myself from the situation and take a restroom break. The time away from this situation is just enough for me to take a few deep breaths, screw on a smile, and resume my discussion. My pre-frontal cortex has overridden my limbic system and reptilian brain. Whew.

6. **Think business at all times.** Your job is to build strategic relationships, not to start budding friendships. You don't want new friends; you want customers or clients. If you focus on understanding and satisfying the business needs of customers and clients, you'll be able to keep personal interests out of the equation. You'll learn more about how to satisfy customer needs in Chapter 6.

7. **Calm yourself down.** This might be an urban legend, but it has been observed by some teachers of psychology and neuroscience. It takes 20 minutes of positive self-talk and breathing to get back into your thinking brain, if you're feeling stirred up or reactive. Just remember, you're always invited to be on the Welcome Wagon team.

8. **Use a Cheater.** If you get anxious talking on the phone with a potential customer, write a bulleted outline of key talking points before your call. Keep to your script and remember to breathe.

Here's another aspect of understanding and facing your fears. Go back to the strengths and challenge exercise in Chapter 2. Look at what you listed as a challenge. If you happened to list fear of public speaking as your main challenge, you probably experience a cortex flip (this happens when your thinking brain goes offline) at the thought of giving a talk in public. In the short term, you can use two ways to deal with this challenge. Remind yourself your thinking brain is offline. Use self-talk to calm yourself down. I am not telling you to go out tomorrow and give a talk in front of 50 people. You can learn to calm your reactive state and hopefully be able to face your fear.

⇆ FEAR OF SELLING QUESTIONNAIRE

The following questionnaire will help you understand just how fearful you are of selling (we'll deal with fear of networking in detail in Chapter 4). When I say selling, I'm referring to any one-on-one activity you do, which results in someone purchasing a product or service from you. So, how fearful are you of selling? Let's find out.

Check one box in each row, which best describes how you feel in different sales situations.

Selling: How Fearful Are You?

Check one box in each row that best describes how you feel in different sales situations.

	Been there, done that – no big deal.	I feel nervous but I've got it under control.	I feel nervous, sick to my stomach, but I do it.	I'm breaking out in a sweat just thinking about it and I'm not going to do it.
1. Making a sales presentation to a small group				
2. Giving a talk at a conference or seminar				
3. Submitting a competitive bid on a job				
4. Writing a project proposal for a customer				
5. Cold-calling a prospect				
6. Talking to a known prospect on the phone				
7. Asking prospective customers if they want to meet rather than suggesting a specific time to meet				
8. Convincing a skeptical prospect of the value of your service or product				
9. Knowing when to end a sales encounter, if there is no prospect of a sale				
10. Overcoming objections to your sales pitch				
11. Closing the sale (buy, sign contract, etc.)				

Fears of Selling and What to Do with Them

Rows 1 and 2 are two of the most common fears related to speaking in public: making a sales presentation to a small group and giving a talk at a conference or seminar. Now, write one suggestion to help overcome your fear of speaking in public.

_____

_____

Rows 3 and 4 address the challenges involved in writing for business. A customer wants you to competitively bid on a job and asks you to write a proposal for a project. Write one suggestion to help you overcome your fears of business writing.

_____

_____

Rows 5 and 6 are two common phone fears: cold calling a prospect and talking on the phone to a prospect you know. Write one suggestion to help you overcome your phone fears.

_____

_____

Rows 7 and 8 ask you to evaluate how convincing you are (being vague vs. being specific): asking a prospective customer to suggest a time and place to meet face-to-face and convincing a skeptical prospect of the value of your service or product. Write one suggestion you have to help you be more self-assured and assertive in these situations.

_____

_____

Rows 9, 10, and 11 deal with being aware of customer needs versus your need: knowing when to end a sales encounter, if there is no prospect of a sale; overcoming objections to your sales pitch; closing the sale. Write one suggestion to help you focus on the customer (hint: in Chapter 6 you'll learn all about understanding and addressing customer needs).

_____

_____

⇋ FEAR OF FEES QUESTIONNAIRE

See how fearful or fearless you are when the time comes to discuss fees.

Fear of Fees

For this questionnaire, I'm using the terms fees and price interchangeably. Check one box in each row that best describes how you feel when discussing fees.

	No	Sometimes	Often	Always
1. Do you feel like you do not have enough experience to justify your fee?				
2. Do you ask your customers if they think your fees are reasonable?				
3. Are you afraid you are not charging enough?				
4. If you state your fee, are you afraid the customer will say no?				
5. If a customer balks at your fee, do you drop the price?				
6. Are you afraid you are charging too much?				
7. In general, do you feel nervous about discussing fees?				
8. If, at the start of a sales pitch, the customer asks about your fees, do you have a strategy to defer the conversation until you finish your presentation?				
9. Did your family of origin speak openly and in a healthy way about money and finances?				
10. Did your family of origin openly and fearfully discuss money or finances?				

Let's go a little deeper.

Rows 1, 2, and 3 address self doubt. If you checked *Often* or *Always* more than *Sometimes* or *No*, then it's time for some self-talk. Here's an example that might help you with self doubt. I was coaching a young woman, Natalie, who recently graduated with a doctoral degree in physical therapy. She wanted to open a private practice and had no idea where to start. She was filled with self-doubt. One goal of coaching was for Natalie to confront her doubts. We made a list of her self-doubts.

1. I'm too young (age wise) to be taken seriously.

2. I don't have enough experience.

3. I'm not sure I can really help people.

We addressed each of these self-doubts by replacing these negative messages with positives ones. "Too young to be taken seriously," was replaced with, "As a recent graduate, I know the latest and most advanced physical therapy methods." Instead of "I don't have enough experience," she said, "I have to remember I interned and trained at two top hospitals in the country." For, "I'm not really sure I can help people," she substituted, "I bring a lot of passion to what I do, which will engage patients."

Two years after Natalie finished coaching with me, I sent her an email and asked her how she was doing. She said three months earlier she opened a physical therapy practice with a colleague from graduate school. She was treating patients and loving it.

Take a minute and write a message to yourself which would build your self-confidence.

_____

_____

_____

Rows 4 and 5 address fear of rejection. If you checked Often or All of the Time more than Sometimes or No, then it's another opportunity for self-talk. It's easy to find yourself going in a downward spiral after a prospective customer says no. Now, you're probably making up many of stories in your head about why this particular person did not buy your product or service. Imagine you are in a situation and a potential customer says no to you. List two stories you might make up about why this person did not buy.

Story #1:

_____

_____

_____

_____

Story #2:

_____

_____

_____

_____

Customers purchase products and services for all sorts of reasons. Many times their decision not to purchase has **nothing at all** to do with you. It's a fact; you'll be confronted with rejection throughout your career. It's important to reassure yourself.

Rows 6, 7, 8, 9, and 10 address anxiety about discussing money. If you checked Often or All of the Time more than Sometimes or No, then it's time to talk money. Here's an example. When I first started out consulting, my only reference point for how much to charge was based on my experience at a large consulting firm. I could not charge anywhere near what they charged. I ruminated over whether I should charge an hourly fee or one fee for the entire project. I had no idea of what those fees would be. I realized I was anxious about talking about fees because no one in my family would talk about money. Remembering this helped me realize why this was hard for me. On the positive side, I knew I had all the credentials and experience that potential clients wanted. I then knew I could face my fears and discuss fees with my clients. What helped me was understanding the reason it was hard for me and using positive self-talk.

Now, it's your turn to think about one way to overcome your fear of discussing money (if you have one).

_____

_____

_____

_____

Here are some general suggestions for you to overcome your fear of fees. When you read through the list of suggestions, keep in mind that some of the suggestions can be used to overcome your fear of selling, too.

1. **State your fee and shut up.** Don't justify your fee or over-talk yourself. Let the customer respond. Keep this discussion as short as possible.
2. **Stick to your guns.** Do not sell yourself short by dropping your fee. In a moment of panic and in desperation to make the sale, all sorts of thoughts are racing through your mind. You know how much time, energy, and money it took to bring your product or service to market. Leave no room for negotiation.
3. **Take a sales training course.** Sometimes, I recommend that my clients attend a short sales training course. I'm not referring to 2-hour sales training seminars designed to lure you into purchasing a costly training package. In fact, I have some reservations about sales training courses. First, most of what is taught is common sense, just neatly packaged in a step-by-step methodology. Some sales training courses focus on the techniques used by the course leader. These leaders tend to be somewhat charismatic and the focus is on the leader, not you. Second, many sales training courses use their own jargon, which might be off-putting to you. Third, unless specifically tailored to your profession or business, general sales training courses might not offer specific industry-related insight or buyer behavior patterns. Fourth, some sales training courses offer a plethora of tips, tactics, and ideas. This might be the case of too much information. If you do want to take a sales training course, I recommend you consult your professional or business association. See what they have to offer. Weigh the time, cost, and energy you spend on taking a course against the benefits you might get. See what happens.
4. **Get a mentor or a coach.** Mentors are individuals who are willing to assist you at no cost. Mentors tend to be senior executives or retirees. Many communities around the country have mentoring programs sponsored by local business councils. Coaches charge you by the hour. Whichever you choose, getting a mentor or coach is probably the best way to get a handle on how to discuss fees. It's been my experience the best mentors are those in businesses not related to yours. Even though they do not have your industry-specific information and experience, they do know how to do the most important

> Get yourself a mentor; it's the best business investment you'll make. And, you won't have to pay!

thing you need: discussing fees and closing deals. You'll get a fresh perspective on selling. Caveat: Look online and you'll see many organizations that offer coaching certification. Before you hire a coach, check out his or her certification. Does the credential seem credible? Will the coach let you talk to current or former clients?

5. **Chitchat first, do business second.** Let's go back to *Critical Connections'* main premise: Marketing is the management of strategic relationships. Here's an extreme example of chitchat first, do business second.

I was introduced to an executive at a multi-national corporation who was in charge of its employee assistance program, a service which helps employees deal with personal problems that might negatively affect their job performance or health. My goal was to get a contract with the corporation to provide a turnkey employee assistance program solution. He suggested we meet for dinner to discuss the proposal. My manager happened to mention this individual was formerly a professional football player. This was all the ammunition I needed to make this dinner a success. I began dinner by commenting on how big his Super Bowl ring was. For the entire meal, we talked football. He loved it. It was all about him. Not once did we talk business. After dinner, on the way out to the car, he leaned over to me and asked if I would send him a proposal.

The message to you is simple. Find out what the other person is interested in and get them to talk about it. Chitchat first, business second.

Now you have tips and tactics to use so you won't sell yourself short.

CHAPTER 4

Networking for Introverts

All of us introverts aspire to be more outgoing, but it's not in our nature.
When I was nearly 50, I discovered that the best thing to do was to tell everyone
I worked with that I'm just shy. People are not mind readers – you need to let
them know.

—Douglas Conant

Artie, a 51-year-old freelance information technology (IT) management consultant had a productive, but somewhat unsatisfying, career as a project manager at a global IT firm. He got to travel overseas, worked on innovative projects, and still had time to spend with his family. He was well respected and was an integral part of the firm. He was recognized as a rising star by top management.

> You don't have to be an introvert to get something useful from this chapter.

However, Artie's work situation was not ideal for him. He worked on most of his projects with a team of engineers. He spent too much time in what he refers to as, "interminably unproductive meetings." When in a staff meeting, he would feel impatient and could not wait for the meeting (whether he was conducting it or not) to end.

To make matters worse, Artie couldn't find any time for himself when he traveled. Whether he was on a plane, driving to the client's site, or having dinner, he was constantly surrounded by his team. He affectionately referred to his team as The Pack. He felt pressure to be part of the pack.

The stress of being surrounded by colleagues was beginning to make him miserable. He told me he felt "peopled-out." He began to think more and more that he might fare better in his work life if he went off on his own and become a freelance consultant.

Artie is a classic introvert – the person you would label shy. If you talked one-on-one with him, you would never know he's an introvert. His warm smile and engaging personality exudes confidence and professionalism. Put him in a networking event and he crumbles like a cookie hitting the floor.

According to Susan Cain in *Quiet: The Power of Introverts in a World That Can't Stop Talking* (Crown Publishers, 2012), introverts like Artie tend to:

- Feel "just right" with less stimulation,

- Would rather take a vacation at the beach and relax with a book than go on a cruise,

- Work carefully and deliberately,

- Wish they were home when in social settings,

- Devote limited social energy to close friends, colleagues, and family.

When Artie first started his information technology consulting business, he was repeatedly told about the benefits and importance of attending networking events. His friends and colleagues said, "It's what you do as a business person." "It's where your customers and referral sources are." "Here's where you make yourself known." Artie agreed.

Hearing this advice, Artie went to the internet and looked up tips on networking. There was no lack of tips, tactics, and techniques to use to play the networking game. After searching online, Artie decided if everyone was doing it (attending networking events), it must be the right thing to do.

After attending several anxiety-provoking networking events, Artie retreated into his shell where he felt safe and secure. So much for Artie attending networking events. Artie needed help.

Out of desperation, Artie came to me and wanted to know how to build his consulting practice. He was ambivalent about trying the networking route again. He wanted to know if he could build his business without attending networking events. Before I was ready to give my advice, I asked him three questions:

Question #1: How do you feel about attending a networking event?

His answer: Very anxious.

Question #2: Given your quiet nature, how many people can you realistically make meaningful contact with at a networking event?

His answer: 1 or 2.

Question #3: Wouldn't you rather be talking one-on-one than working the room?

His answer: Yes.

I told Artie I had some strategies he could use to deal with his anxiety about attending networking events.

The first step was to breakdown Artie's networking strategy into three manageable tasks.

Task #1: Identify Strengths and Challenges

I worked with him to identify and articulate his biggest strengths and most difficult challenges. Artie immediately focused on his biggest challenge: fear of networking. I knew if we went into detail talking about this challenge, Artie would tumble down a rabbit hole of anxiety. I quickly shifted the topic away from his challenge. I asked Artie, "What is your key strength?" He perked up and said, "writing," whether it was writing term papers in college, writing business proposals, or writing short articles in professional publications.

Okay, now we're getting somewhere. "Let's work on using your key strength to promote your consulting business."

Task #2: Leverage Your Key Strength

For Artie it was crystal clear: writing. Artie agreed to write one short article called *The Future Implications of Big Data.* He would write this article for an online IT ezine (lucky for Artie, the editor of this ezine was an old friend from graduate school). The article was published two months after he submitted it. This was his first step to establishing himself as an expert. He put the stake in the ground as an authority on "big data." A bold move to get started.

Task #3: Expand Your Strength

Artie understood the value of getting out and meeting people. From my experiences, I've found word-of-mouth referrals and presenting papers at conferences and seminars are the best vehicles for generating work. This somewhat academic approach to networking works best for promoting professional services.

Artie sent a proposal to present his article *The Future Implications of Big Data* to a regional IT conference where he was chosen to present his paper. His name was listed in the online conference program as a speaker. The conference program announcements and registration forms were posted online and sent via social media to potential registrants. Conference and seminar announcements also were sent via snail mail to potential attendees, sometimes numbering into the thousands. This was a great vehicle for Artie to get visibility. Artie's name began to be seen by more and more potential clients.

The key to Artie's continuing success was to break down ideas and tasks into small, manageable bites. This was a good way for him to prevent task-overload.

What About You?

Now it's your turn to think about your networking strategy. Start planning your networking strategy after you've completed the Strength and Challenges exercises in Chapter 2.

> **Key point:** lead with your strengths, not your challenges. Why would you expose yourself to needless anxiety? If you see networking events as an anxiety-provoking experience, try something else more suited to you.

Introverts can take advantage of what Malcolm Gladwell calls Connectors. Connectors are those people in your community who know large numbers of people and who are great at making introductions (from *The Tipping Point: How Little Things Can Make a Big Difference*). Connectors are all about people and are eager to share their list of contacts. You can spot a Connector across the room. This is the person you see scrolling through their list of contacts on their smart phone looking for the right connection for the right person. The Connector solves problems by making connections. "I know this guy" . . . "you should definitely meet this woman" . . . "if this guy can't help you, try so-and-so."

What more can an introvert want? I introduced Artie to a Connector, Rachel. I knew Rachel because she attended one of my marketing workshops. I was impressed with how wide a net Rachel cast over her local business community. I guess in some way I was a Connector this time.

Artie met Rachel the Connector for lunch. Prior to lunch, Rachel prepared a list of 17 people and local organizations for Artie to contact. After lunch, Artie called me bubbling with excitement. He now had a comfortable place to start. Artie now stays in touch with Rachel and has begun to introduce Rachel to his business contacts.

If you attend a small seminar or workshop, you'll probably be asked at some point to introduce yourself to the other participants. This is a great opportunity to make yourself known, in a non-threatening setting. You'll probably have to tweak your elevator speech or power message to meet the needs of the type of group; you're going to learn all about elevator speeches and power messages in Chapter 5. Breakfasts, lunches, seminars, and conferences provide great opportunities to meet one-on-one and to connect with others.

> **Key point:** Whether you are attending a networking event or having a one-on-one meeting, your goal is to develop a business relationship, not to make friends. You need customers, not friends.

No one is dragging you kicking and screaming, but networking events might be where the money is. Here are some suggestions about how to network in your own, introverted way:

1. Write a game plan prior to the event and identify specific individuals to meet. Keep your networking goal in mind and at the same time be flexible (See plan outline below).

2. Get the jump on other attendees before the event by volunteering with the sponsoring organization to do anything. Help with on-site registration. Prepare

or serve refreshments. Sponsor a door prize (for example, a Starbucks gift card). This is a great way to meet the leaders of the organization sponsoring the event.

3. Do not get distracted by talking to friends or those not in a position to help you.

4. Practice your elevator speech (See Chapter 5). When you meet someone at a networking event, you have a few precious seconds to tell your story. Be ready to modify your story on the fly based on the special interests of the person you are talking with. Bottom line: make your elevator speech short and sweet.

5. When you make contact with people at a networking event, be sure to ask them if they know any other individuals you should meet. And, ask people you meet for the names of other networking events.

6. Determine how you want to end this brief conversation. What kind of follow-up do you want? Ask for a meeting; get a business card; give your business card; or invite the person to attend another event.

7. Know when to bail out. Trust your instincts and you'll know when to leave.

Your Personalized Networking Plan

Set a goal of meeting one or two potential customers or those in position to refer business to you. Remember Rachel the Connector.

1. Find three free local or regional networking events, their dates and locations.

2. Go online and find names of either companies or individuals who will be attending. If this event is sponsored by a professional or civic organization, get the names of key individuals who will be there.

3. As mentioned above, contact the event coordinator at each networking event and ask to volunteer to do something at the event, such as handing out name tags or helping with setting up refreshments.

4. Keep a log or database of those you talked to and the result of the conversation.

Before the Event

Name of Event	Date	Location	Two People to Meet	Volunteer to
			1. 2.	
			1. 2.	
			1. 2.	

After the Event

Name of Event	People to Follow-up	Goal of follow-up

Congratulations, you have ventured unscathed into the land of networking.

So, what happened to Artie? He continues to publish his articles online and has become a respected blogger in the IT community. And, he's making a comfortable living from his consulting. Good work, Artie.

It may seem extroverts rule, but theirs isn't the only successful way to network. If you are an introvert, it's possible to find your own way of networking, which is suited to your quiet strengths and talents.

Are you an introvert? Find out at www. thepowerofintroverts. com

CHAPTER 5

What Do You Say
In and Out of an Elevator?

In reading this chapter, you'll learn the best ways to connect with potential referrers and how to engage potential customers or clients with the goal of building a relationship. By the end of this chapter, you'll have created an elevator speech for referrers and a power message for potential customers. Along the way, you'll learn tons of tips and practical tools to make your elevator speech and power message deliver more maximum impact.

The Elevator Speech

An "elevator speech" is something you say to potential referral sources, which briefly describes your business. A referral source is an individual in a position to refer clients or customers to you. The elevator speech is usually used in-person when meeting someone for the first time. In Chapter 8, we'll go into more detail about how important referral sources are in generating business for you. Depending on whom you are talking to, you'll want to create several versions of your elevator speech.

There are two main types of elevator speeches. The first type is used for those working in any type of organization. The goal of the elevator speech in this context is to inform others about a project you are working on which, in some way, might impact them and others in the organization. For example, your organization is going to implement a new quality control program. You know word-of-mouth is the best way to communicate with others about this new program. When you bump into another employee, you would start with a brief description of this project. You would stress the value and benefit of the project. And finally, you would ask for support for the project.

The second type of elevator speech is aimed at potential referral sources. This is a brief statement describing your business. The goal of this type of elevator speech is to establish a strategic relationship with the other person. This is the type of elevator speech we'll be working on.

My Foray into the Elevator

Many years ago, I met an elderly gentleman at my cousin's wedding. The gentleman told me he used to work in the "rag trade" in New York City's garment industry. He said he sold women's dresses to department stores in and around New York City. I immediately knew what he was talking about and what he did for a living. He told me what he did in two sentences and I got it. Then, he asked me what I did. I proceeded to muddle through a description about what I did. I don't remember exactly what I said, but it sounded something like, "I develop and implement strategic and tactical marketing programs for health care delivery systems." I sounded like a bumbling idiot. After I finished, which seemed like an eternity, he stepped back, scratched his head in bewilderment, and said, "But Evan, what do you sell?" I was floored.

⇄

"But Evan, what do you sell?"

At this time, I had never heard of an elevator speech (some call it an *elevator pitch*). Nowadays, you hear the term elevator speech used all the time. You hear sales trainers say, "You must have an elevator speech in order to pitch your product or service. You must have a ready-made answer to the question, 'What do you do?'"

The idea of an elevator speech is that you should be able to communicate a brief summary of what you do in the time span of an elevator ride. When I think of a speech, my mind automatically flashes to a politician standing on a podium giving an impassioned or long-winded speech to a bunch of constituents. We are not giving speeches; we are initiating a business dialogue with the goal of having the other person purchase our product or service. The term *elevator pitch* is even worse. When I hear the word "pitch," I'm reminded of this guy on late-night cable television pitching his super duper cleaning product or some magic weight loss pill. We are not pitching; we are initiating a business dialogue with the result of developing a referral relationship. I do not like either expression, but I generally use "elevator speech."

Your Elevator Speech

You hear so-called experts say your elevator speech should take no more than two or three minutes. Others say it should take no more than ninety seconds. Others recommend thirty seconds and some people say it should be no longer than fifteen to twenty seconds. I didn't realize you have to have a stopwatch on hand when you give your elevator speech. I've even heard you should limit your words to thirteen. Why thirteen, why not fifteen? Do we really want to get mired down by limiting ourselves to length of speech and or number of words?

I do not recommend using fill-in-the-blanks forms. Why? Because, you are unique. You have something special to offer referral sources and customers. You can't make yourself fit into someone else's mold. You can't express your uniqueness using a canned format.

Meeting new people can be anxiety provoking. You can't deliver an elevator speech in a warm and welcoming way, if your limbic system is in an uproar. In Chapter 3, I talked about the role of your brain when faced with potential fears. The brain stem signals there is danger, the limbic system gets activated, and emotions are expressed in response to the real or imaginary danger. Before you create your personalized elevator speech, be aware that at some point during your "speech," you might get emotionally activated.

Here's the way I use elevator speeches. When I meet someone who is a potential referral source, I'll use my elevator speech as a tool to introduce myself and tell them what I do and how I can help. You can adapt your elevator speech to fit in your website or Facebook business page. You don't have to re-invent the wheel. If you have a section of your website that directly addresses the needs of referrers, then by all means use your elevator speech.

In Chapter 7, we'll meet the jargon police whose role is to monitor your use of jargon. Using jargon in your elevator speech and power message is a big turn-off for those listening to you. Jargon includes all of the words you use that are unique to your business. When you use jargon there is a good chance the person listening to you will not understand what you are saying. This is not a good way to make a first impression.

At a local networking event, I overheard a psychotherapist talking to a lawyer – a potential referrer. The therapist thought the lawyer might have clients with emotional or relationship problems. In this case, the therapist was trolling for referrals. The therapist said to the lawyer, "I do psychotherapy, Gestalt Therapy, Trauma-Focused Cognitive Behavioral Therapy, and Premarital Counseling." You see what I'm talking about? The jargon police would have had a field day with this elevator speech. You might want to gently and infrequently use minimal jargon if you are talking to someone who is in your industry or profession.

The very first thing to consider when you are approaching a prospect is whether the person you will be talking with is actually in a position to move business your way. In strict sales parlance, you are preparing to "qualify your prospect." You want to know the likeliness of this prospect being in a position to refer business your way. You'll learn which questions to ask and how to determine if a potential referrer is a good prospect for referrals in Chapter 7.

Time to create your own elevator speech. There are five parts to your elevator speech:

1. What do I sell?

2. Sound bite

3. The pain or problem I address

4. Sweet spot

5. Closing

Over time, you'll want to modify or refine your elevator speech. Just as you reprint your business card when you move or get a new address or phone number, you have to refresh your elevator speech. Use the worksheet on page 70 to write down as much as you need to accurately fill in each of the following parts.

Part One: Ask Yourself, "What Do I Sell?"

"What is the product or service I'm selling?" Do not limit yourself to a certain number of words. Keep this part of your elevator speech in your head. This is a way to ground yourself before you talk to anyone. If you are promoting two different products or services, then think of two different ideas for two different pitches.

For example, I am a marketing consultant and a customer service training consultant. These are two very different services. If I think about both of them in the first part of my elevator speech and integrate the two into the body of my elevator speech, it will sound confusing. The person listening to me will not be able to figure out how I can help him. A prospective referral source who knows a client in need of a marketing plan, probably has no interest in hiring me to conduct customer service training. Make it easy for the potential referrer. Stick to one service or product when preparing Part One. This is easier said than done. You are passionate about what you can offer and want to share your enthusiasm with all.

Part Two: My Sound Bite

This is what you say to any potential referral source who will listen. This part is all about you.

1. **Say your name.** If you are a physician, dentist, or have a PhD or other doctorate degree, you might want to consider introducing yourself by saying, "I'm John Doe and I am a dentist," vs. "I'm Dr. Doe." Keep your introduction informal.

2. **State your professional credentials.** If you think stating your professional degree or credential will help establish or enhance your credibility, then do so. If not, don't say it.

3. **Give the location of where you work (city or town).** If you do some work out-of-town or overseas, say it, too.

4. **Say how long you've been doing what you're doing.** This is tricky in two ways. One, if you're just starting your own business, you don't want the prospective referrer to think of you as a rookie with little or no prior experience. You can say something like, "For the past 15 years I've worked as an interior designer at a large furniture store. Now I have my own interior design business." Second, what do you say if you are starting a second or maybe a third career or business? My advice: be honest. Be upfront and say something like, "I was employed in the aerospace industry but now I'm

working as a freelance photographer." Remember, you have plenty of real-life experience and wisdom, which can increase your credibility.

Part Three: The Pain or Problem I Address

This part of your elevator speech has nothing to do with what you do. This idea is often surprising to people. It's all about your ability to identify and relate to the pain or problem facing prospective customers. Even though you are talking to a prospective referrer, you still need to assure the referrer you are tuned into their customers' pain or problem. My suggestion is if you have more than one pain or problem to address, just pick one to discuss. You don't want to dilute the impact of the main problem you address. This part must be jargonless.

Sometimes, I start this section with, "Small business owners come to me when their marketing efforts have stalled out or they're losing business to competitors." Remember, this section is not about you.

Part Four: My Sweet Spot

The term sweet spot refers to an area on a baseball bat where the most effective contact is made with the ball. The sweet spot is the most important part of your elevator speech. You tell the other person what makes you special or different in what you offer. It's at this time you amp up your excitement and passion about what you do and why you're special. Once again, couch your sweet spot in terms of "what's in it for the referrer." Repeat after me: Communicate my passion. It is my sweet spot. This part should be jargonless.

Part Five: My Closing

Your closing is the most difficult part of your elevator speech. I prefer to call the closing, Landing the Plane. You can't land the plane safely if your limbic system is in an uproar. In my marketing workshops, I have heard successful business owners and novices alike hesitate when they practice their elevator speech in front of workshop participants.

↺

Land the plane smoothly.

Why is landing the plane so difficult for some people? Why do competent people get flustered? Some people hesitate landing the plane due to their fear of rejection. Landing the plane requires you to be open, honest, and direct with the other person. You are asking for something. You might balk at the need to plan your landing. However, you learned some skills in Chapter 3 on how to overcome such fears.

One more concern. What happens if during the landing process, you experience the dreaded awkward silence? It's perfectly okay to wait a few seconds without conversation. This is a good time for you to take a deep breath and remember some of the options you have at your disposal. This type of self-talk will help you calm down your amygdala.

Here are some options for you to use when landing the plane, depending on the situation.

- Ask for a meeting if you think the potential referrer can turn into a strategic relationship. Face-to-face is preferable. Phone is okay.

- Exchange business cards if you would like to keep this person in your database of contacts.

- Make a LinkedIn, Facebook, Twitter or other social media request. It's the thing to do.

- If you know about local seminars, conferences, or workshops, which might be of interest, invite him or her.

- If you do nothing else, just exchange business cards.

Here are some examples of ways to turn your hesitant (wimpy) response into a more self-assured (direct) response.

Don't Wimp Out!

Wimpy	Direct
Can I call you?	When can I call you?
Do you have a business card?	I'd like your business card.
Can I have your email address?	What's your email address?
Maybe we should have lunch?	When can we have lunch?
Can I be a Contact in LinkedIn?	I'll make contact with you on LinkedIn.

⇆ TIME FOR A QUICK QUIZ

Be honest with your answers.

Question 1: Right now, how many of your own business cards do you have in your wallet, purse, or brief case? _____

If you have more than five, you pass Part 1 of the quiz. If you have fewer than five, you better put more of your business cards in your wallet, purse or briefcase or have more printed.

Question 2: How many of your own business cards do you have lying around your house? _____

If you have more than fifty, then you pass Part 2 of the quiz. If you have fewer than fifty, stop reading this book, go online now, and order more business cards.

Question 3: This requires a *yes* or *no* answer.

I have up-to-date business cards. ○ YES ○ NO

If you answered No, you know what to do.

What is the big deal about having business cards? Key point: Your elevator speech is your business card in action. Along with having a prepared elevator speech, you should always have up-to-date business cards on hand. I was recently at a business networking event. I met a lawyer who specializes in working with small business owners on legal matters. He was the perfect referral source for me. I wanted to follow up with him and at the end of our brief conversation I asked him for his business card. He fished through his wallet and found a crumpled up, dog-eared business card. He took out the card and said, "Oh, my phone number changed, and so did my email address." He scribbled the new contact information on the back of his card and handed it to me. I then thought twice about contacting him. I decided there must be other lawyers like him without crumpled, outdated business cards.

⇆

Your elevator speech is your business card in action.

I did not contact him. You know what they say about first impressions. Is this the kind of first impression you want to make?

Tips for creating a readable and informative business card.

1. Put your contact information on only one side of your card.

2. Size of font is important. If your customers are over age 50, pump up the size of the font.

3. Put the least amount of contact information on your card. Do you need to put your landline, cell, fax, email address, and website on the card?

4. Make sure any graphic you use does not overshadow your contact information.

5. Buy small quantities even though you get price discounts when you order more.

Let's review the key elements of an effective elevator speech.

1. Introduce yourself.

2. Give a brief sound bite on what pain or types of problems you address.

3. Hit your sweet spot by briefly telling (not explaining) what makes you special in your offering.

4. Be sure to express your passion.

5. End by landing the plane. What sort of follow-up do you want? If you only do one thing, get the other person's business contact information for your database.

⇄ Elevator Speech for Referrers Worksheet

#1. Name the product or service I'm selling:

_____

_____

_____

#2. My Sound Bite:

_____

_____

_____

#3. The Pain or Problem I Address:

_____

_____

_____

#4. My Sweet Spot:

_____

_____

_____

#5. My Closing:

_____

_____

_____

Now, condense, edit, delete, or add what you need. Put your elevator speech all together.

_____

_____

_____

_____

_____

_____

_____

_____

_____

Count the number of jargon words used in your elevator speech. Replace them with common words. Say your elevator speech to friends who are not familiar with your business. Ask them if there are any technical words or phrases they are not familiar with. Your friends can become your backup jargon police.

Your elevator speech is ready to go. Remember; be flexible and prepared to adapt it on the spot.

Power Message

Your power message is what you say to potential customers or clients. This generally takes place on the phone. The same power message format should be used when talking in front of another person.

Why do I need both an elevator speech and a power message? Why can't I say the same thing to both referrers and prospective clients? Important note: Your power message is not an elevator speech. Use your power message when a potential client wants to know what you do and how you can help them. Focus on what you do within the context of what is in it for the potential client.

The power message has three parts. One is about you. The second part is about what's in it for the prospect. The third part is landing the plane. Your power message is less scripted than your elevator speech.

What do you say if a prospect initially asks you how much you charge? I call this type of prospect a shopper. First, do not answer the question. Second, do not launch into your power message. Ask a few benign questions such as, "What are you looking for? Have you talked to others in the same business?" If you are unable to redirect the conversation back to the other person, then quickly land the plane by simply stating your fee (or a range of fees). Try once more to turn the conversation back to the customer. Shoppers shop for bargains. You are not a bargain-basement store.

Is it okay to use jargon in your power message? It depends on who the customer is and how much knowledge he or she has about your business. It may be fine to use some jargon with a customer who knows your business. If you have a customer unfamiliar with your business, the moment you start to use jargon, you will lose the customer's attention. The conversation automatically shifts back to you instead of focusing on the prospect's needs.

⇄ Your power message is aimed at the type of client who will contact you the most often.

In this case, you wind up describing things the prospect can't connect with and she might not understand what you are saying.

Here are some tips to make your power message powerful.

- Don't tell the caller what you **don't** do. Frame all conversations in a positive way.

- Your power message can be modified to fit your website, online business presence, other online professional listings, or additional promotional information.

- Practice your message. **Write it down** and **say it out loud.**

- Have someone listen to your power message. Ask him or her to give you feedback. Ask for one thing he liked about your message and one technical suggestion he might have for you. Let him become your jargon police.

Now it's time to write your power message. Aim your thinking towards the person most likely to purchase your product or service. For example, I worked with a fitness studio to create a new marketing program. One objective of the marketing plan was to get prospective clients to call the studio for a complimentary session. The owner was targeting men over age 50 who had metabolic syndromes (Metabolic syndromes are clusters of conditions – increased blood pressure, a high blood sugar level, excess body fat around the waist and abnormal cholesterol levels – that occur together, increasing risk of heart disease, stroke and diabetes. From www.mayoclinic.org). We worked together to create a power message specifically geared to this segment of the market.

POWER MESSAGE EXAMPLE

My name is Meg B. and I'm the manager at Fitness Strength & Training in Any City, USA. I have been a personal trainer for the past 11 years and have a Bachelor's Degree from Penn State in Kinesiology. I've worked with cancer patients, elite athletes, and many weight-loss clients. Fitness Strength & Training is a unique fitness studio because you receive a personalized exercise experience, nutrition coaching, and most importantly, accountability. All of our training sessions are conducted one-on-one in semi-private rooms to eliminate distraction. We help people realize their true potential as we coach them towards a healthier lifestyle.

"Here's my business card. I'd be happy to offer you one complimentary training session. See the other side of the business card for details. Also, I'd like your contact information so I can send you our newsletter."

Key points:

• Notice this power message contained the three parts discussed previously:
  1. Information about the trainer.
  2. Information geared to helping the client.
  3. A strong landing or closing.

• This power message is only 139 words. She said what was needed and stopped.

• A power message is not as structured as an elevator speech. Meg clearly articulated the goal of training: a healthier lifestyle. It's the "What's in it for me (the client)" part of the message and she smoothly, in a self-assured way, landed the plane.

⇆ CREATE YOUR PERSONALIZED POWER MESSAGE

In the space below, write free-flowing ideas, thoughts, etc. about what you want to tell your prospective client or customer about your product or service. Select key points. Write as much as you want. Do not hold back. Be sure to land the plane.

_____

_____

_____

_____

_____

_____

_____

_____

_____

_____

_____

_____

Look at what you wrote above and see if you included the three components. Delete one-half of what you wrote. Yes, one half.

_____

_____

_____

_____

_____

Write any jargon or technical words here.

_____

_____

_____

_____

_____

Now write your final version of your power message.

_____

_____

_____

_____

_____

_____

_____

Getting to the Right Person with the Right Message

In many cases, it's not easy to talk directly to the person in a position to purchase your product or service. Sometimes, you wind your way through myriad people until you finally talk with one person who can make the decision. Who are these people? They are referred to as **Gatekeepers, Influencers & Users, Deciders, and Buyers**. If you decided not to include a Buyer Power Message since these people are not directly involved in hiring consultants or make purchasing decisions, you'll want to have a plan on how to approach each of these folks.

Gatekeepers

In order to get access to a potential referrer who works in a large corporation or a small company or agency, you need to work your way past gatekeepers. These people are sentinels. Their job is to keep vendors, like you, at bay and restrict access to the potential referrer. There might be additional gatekeepers throughout the organization who restrict access to others involved in the decision-making process.

Your objective is to make the gatekeeper feel at ease with you. Here are some tips on how to get the gatekeeper to open the gate for you. These tips should be viewed as a way to help you through these initial awkward conversations. Be flexible. There is no sure-fire way to do this.

1. After you introduce yourself, say something like, "Can you help me?" Or, "Can you steer me in the right direction? How can I find Mr. John Smith?"

2. Next, you might be asked the dreaded question, "What's this regarding?" If someone has referred you, be forthcoming and mention this person by name. If no one has referred you, then pull out your elevator speech.

3. If the gatekeeper does not hang up on you, ask when is the best time to call back and talk directly to the potential referrer. Or, ask for an email address.

4. At the end of the conversation, you might add, "Can you please tell me your name, again?"

Influencers & Users

These folks do not make the actual decision to purchase your product or service. However, they do exert influence on those who make the final purchasing decision. Think of them as having:

• Technical knowledge and expertise related to your product or service. They are sometimes called content or subject matter experts.

• Direct access to the decision maker.

• Direct experience with the product or service you are selling.

You might have to work your way through a Gatekeeper to get to Influencers. One way to build a relationship with an Influencer is to use just enough jargon to communicate the message that you are an "insider." Yes, you read this correctly. I did contradict myself. It's okay to use jargon in this instance.

I like to build relationships with Influencers by sharing technical information with them. For instance, one Influencer I met at a networking event was a graphic designer who works for a large advertising agency. While I was talking with her, I realized that her advertising agency would make a perfect client for me. I quickly thought I should get in to see the advertising agency's CEO and discuss how my client retention training program would benefit the agency.

During the networking event, the graphic designer and I were commiserating about the ineffectiveness of PowerPoint presentations. While we were talking, I remembered reading a monograph entitled *The Cognitive Style of PowerPoint: Pitching Out Corrupts Within* by Edward Tufte (Graphic Press, 2011). This essay focused on the limitations of PowerPoint. I told her about this monograph and said I would send her a copy. I went home, opened Amazon on my computer, purchased the monograph, and had it in her hands two days later. A great way to build a strategic relationship.

End of story. I talked to the graphic designer a few weeks later and she got me in to see the CEO. The result was not what I expected. The CEO wanted me to present a talk to his staff on strategic planning, instead of hiring me to conduct my client retention program.

Deciders

Finally we get to the person you've been hunting for – Mr. or Ms. Decider. Yes, this is the keeper of the money, the final authority, the CEO. Now you finally have the opportunity to articulate your Power Message to the most important person. By the time you approach the Decider, you've already done a lot of work to get here.

CHAPTER 6

Know Your Customer

How do you gauge customer satisfaction? How do you get to know what your customers need and what motivates them to purchase? How do you keep customers loyal? In this chapter, you'll discover what your customers need and how to satisfy those needs. We'll discuss the challenges of marketing in a world of diminishing customer loyalty. In addition, we'll explore how customer service and marketing can be one in the same.

Customer service and marketing can be one in the same.

There is an additional perspective on "know your customer." I call this perspective "business blind spots." If you have business blind spots, you don't pay attention to your customers' needs, how satisfied they are, and where your business is coming from. If you suffer from business blind spots, you tend to make assumptions about marketing, customer needs, and satisfaction.

I have developed a number of marketing plans for outpatient diagnostic imaging centers. These centers provide x-ray, CT, MRI, and PET scanning services. The centers rely only on referrals from physicians seeking imaging studies for their patients. The public cannot walk in and request an imaging test. When I asked several imaging center's medical directors who their top referring physician was, their answer was usually inaccurate. They were guessing.

I requested a list of referring physicians from the past year and how many patient referrals each physician made. (Many imaging centers do not track referrals by individual physicians, an identifiable blind spot). I went to work on analyzing the referring physician data. I was able to glean two major facts from the data.

1. The top referrer was not the physician who the medical director thought it was. While at one time this referring physician might have been a top referrer, referral patterns change.

2. A majority of referrals came from six physicians out of a total pool of 37.

I concluded that when it comes time to understand referring physician behavior, it's best to be data-driven rather than assumption driven.

The more I discussed the issue of physician referral patterns, the more curious I got about understanding the referral patterns from the patients' perspective. I talked to the staff at the center about referral issues with patients. The staff indicated they had an excessive amount of no-shows and cancellations. A no-show is defined as a patient who has made an appointment over the phone with the imaging center and does not show up. No shows are different than those who cancel their appointment.

I acquired patient referral statistics and found that of those patients who scheduled an appointment:

- Most of the no-shows occurred around 10:00 a.m.

- Friday was the day of the week with the most no-shows.

- An overwhelming majority of no-shows subscribed to the same insurance carrier.

Why are we talking about this in a book about marketing? Because, this story is a great example of how one question, "Who is your top referrer?" opened the door into understanding a deeper level of customer behavior.

These centers did not understand the needs of their patients. These patients needed reminder phone calls. When reminder calls were made, the no-show rate dramatically decreased.

A Brief Look at Customer Behavior

Moving past the blind spots, let's see what's going on with today's consumers. It is not my intent to compare and contrast old school customers with new school customers. It's too easy to say Baby Boomers (those born between 1946 and 1964) purchase this way and Millennials (those born between 1981 and 2000) purchase another way. However, customers buying patterns and attitudes have been evolving over time. We know that customers today:

1. Want to pay less and expect more for their money.

2. Are getting more and more skeptical about product claims.

3. Are pushing back on traditional sales techniques and shying away from pressure tactics from salespeople.

4. Are demanding clear and tangible value.

The flip side of "know your customer" is having thy customer know you, an important aspect of customer needs. I firmly believe people want to do business with people they know. This is especially true if you're promoting a personal or professional service. When it comes to promoting a product, customers want to know who's standing behind the product they purchase. Take Sir Richard Branson, founder of the Virgin Group. The Virgin Group consists of more than 400 companies. When you see Branson being interviewed on television, he comes across as warm and engaging. He is willing to tell stories about his past. He has a recognizable face. You might even want to have coffee with him. You associate, for example, Virgin Airlines with Sir Richard's face.

What Happened to Customer Loyalty?

Marketing researchers have obsessed about customer loyalty for ages. Large corporations have devised elaborate customer loyalty programs. But things are changing, quickly. Nowadays, customer loyalty is slipping through the fingers of corporations. I sifted through several market research studies on loyalty and brand loyalty. I concluded that when it comes to keeping customers loyal, there is no one magic bullet or best practice.

Here's an example of a customer (me) going from loyal to disloyal. I used to be a loyal customer of United Airlines. I attained the status of Premier Executive, got all the perks, and enjoyed life in business class. Then Southwest entered my local market. Cheap fares, no frills, easy to book. I had reservations (is there a pun somewhere here?) about the cattle-car feeling at Southwest and its policy of using a first-come, first-served seat selection process. Before I switched, I considered what it meant to me to give up my status on United and hop on an all-steerage airline.

When I started writing this chapter, I realized I was Mr. New Consumer. I wanted more for less. Maybe Southwest would give me more for less. Let's see, there were more Southwest flights available at all three of my local airports. Not only were there more flights, but Southwest also flew to more places than United.

Fares were considerably cheaper. To make matters worse with United, I became skeptical when United started limiting perks for frequent flyers. And, I was even more doubtful about the future of this airline when United merged with Continental Airlines. I started to see tangible value by flying Southwest. I decided to switch from United to Southwest. I thought I made a good decision.

To complicate matters about customer loyalty, I recently realized by using one of my credit cards, I could use points accrued from making purchases on my credit card to pay for airfares, hotels, gas, or airline baggage fees. For example, there are credit cards that earn about 2 percent rewards per $1 spent when you redeem for travel. Credit card customers acquire 40,000 (or some other amount) bonus miles when they charge $3,000 worth of purchases within a given time period. This translates into about $400 in travel statement credit. The beauty of using this type of credit card is you are not limited to using any one airline.

What did I do? I closed out my old credit card and signed up for this new one and started accruing points. So much for being a loyal credit card customer. Now I could pay for my Southwest trips using points from my credit card, and get great fares, too.

The story doesn't stop here. In 2008, Airbnb bursts on the scene. According to its website:

> Airbnb is a community marketplace where guests can book spaces from hosts, connecting people who have space to spare with those who are looking for a place to stay. Through their experiences on Airbnb, guests and hosts build real connections with real people from all over the globe.

Airbnb has taken the idea of renting rooms to a whole new level. Prior to booking your room, you can read customer reviews as well as read what the property owners say about past renters.

The arrival of Airbnb type services brings up the key fact about loyalty. Customers now rely more on information about hotels from other customers rather than from the hotel's advertising.

There goes loyalty down the drain.

According to a recent study, there has been a drop in customer's loyalty to hotel brands. Only 8 percent of those polled who stay in hotels said they always book at the same hotel chain. Two reasons for this mass defection might be consumers can quickly find cheaper hotel prices and customer reviews on websites such as Trip Advisor, Kayak, and Trivago. Who wouldn't want to pay less for the same or better quality hotel room? Remember today's customer demands high quality at reasonable prices.

⇇
Customers are on high-alert, searching for the best value for their money. Kiss loyalty goodbye.

Now back to the beleaguered airlines. The market research firm Colloquy found "54 percent of U.S. airline loyalty-program members are 'unhappy' with their reward options." And, 48 percent say they've been "frustrated" by the reward redemption process.

Let's look at the chronology of my story.

- First, I defected from United to Southwest.

- After that, I used up my hotel points.

- Then, I applied my credit card points to pay for hotels or airfares.

- Finally, I switched to using Airbnb properties and paying for it with points from my credit card.

When I began to rely on other people's reviews, I became more and more aware of the impact other customers had on my purchasing decisions. The customer's needs were no longer driven by loyalty, but by quality and value.

A Few Words About Customer Satisfaction Surveys

As important as customer's needs are, customer satisfaction is another essential element of "know your customer." *Critical Connections* is not a guide on how to create customer satisfaction surveys. However, there is a thin line between marketing and customer satisfaction. We are going to cross that thin line and briefly touch on the principles of customer satisfaction and how to measure it. Customer satisfaction surveys solicit feedback from customers to get a sense of how satisfied they are with the service you provide and the quality of your product or service. The information obtained from customers is used to assess and improve customer loyalty.

How do you know what customers need from your product or service? You could ask them. You could observe them. You could guess. What about doing all three? In theory, it sounds like a good idea. But in reality it's not easy. Ask yourself: Would I rather be out promoting my product and making sales or would I rather be writing survey questions and polling customers? The answer is a clear. It depends. If you have time, put together a short survey.

It is interesting to note in the world of healthcare, when patients are asked about the quality of their treatment experience, they tend to express satisfaction or dissatisfaction in terms of the service they received. Patients consider the concept of quality in terms of service. For example, if staff are friendly, courteous, and welcoming, patients will rate the quality of their care in a favorable way.

Eventually, you'll want to use surveys. A short overview of survey methods used to measure customer satisfaction is in the table below, *How to Get to Know Your Customers.* When you're ready to conduct surveys, this table will help you consider the pros and cons of different survey methods, which will help you delve deeper into customer satisfaction.

⇆ HOW TO GET TO KNOW YOUR CUSTOMERS

Survey Method	Pros	Cons
Talk one-on-one informally with customers	• Allows for immediate feedback • Might get more information than you thought • Allows you to make a non-selling personal connection with customer	• Can only talk with a limited number of customers at any one time • You might not get a good cross section of your customer base • Is time consuming
Conduct online customer needs survey* * This is not a customer satisfaction survey.	• Can reach a large number of customers • Easy to do • Minimum cost • Good way to get your name online	• Need to understand the intricacies of how surveys work (there are survey-building websites that can help you create effective surveys) • Takes time to refine survey questions
Conduct focus groups	• Group interaction generates unexpected ideas • Customers appreciate the opportunity to participate • Another way to make a personal connection with customers	• Takes time, energy, and money to organize and conduct the focus group • More effective if conducted by trained focus group facilitator • Might need to conduct more than one focus group, if you service more than one market segment
Search the internet for industry-related data on your customers' purchasing patterns and needs	• Easy to do • Inexpensive • Allows you to dig deeper into your customers' needs	• Data on your industry might not be available • Data might be too global for your local needs • Data might be outdated

However, the latest trend in customer satisfaction is something called Net Promoter Score or NPS. This process employs a streamlined method to measure customer satisfaction. Some organizations ask just one question in order to elicit a customer's NPS. The question posed to the customer might be worded, "How likely is it you would recommend (name of your company) to a colleague or friend?"

NPS uses a ten point rating scale from 0 – 10. Any customer who scores a 9 or 10 is considered a *Promoter*. Promoters are your loyal customers. Those scoring a 7 or 8 are called *Passives*. Even though this group of Passives is happy with you, they can bolt at the drop of a hat. Remember what I said earlier about the demise of loyalty. Those who scored from 0 – 6 are *Detractors*. These are the tough customers you can't please and will most likely say negative things about their experience with you.

You can please some of the people all of the time, you can please all of the people some of the time, but you can't please all of the people all of the time.

—John Lydgate

To determine your NPS, take the percent of your customers who are Promoters and subtract the percentage who are Detractors. After you determine your customers' NPS, you can fine-tune your product or service. Also, you can take a close look at your customers' needs in order to increase customer satisfaction.

⇆ EXAMPLE OF NET PROMOTER SCORE SURVEY QUESTIONNAIRE

Based on your experience, how likely is it that you would recommend a friend to my business?

Very Unlikely										Very Likely
0	1	2	3	4	5	6	7	8	9	10
Detractors							Passives		Promoters	

What improvement can we make in the product or service we provide?

_____

_____

_____

_____

A Deeper Dive into Customer Needs

Once you understand customer needs, you'll be able to create targeted marketing strategies and tactics based on need. The key to understanding customer need is to focus on the customer, not yourself. This might sound like common sense. Think about it. Are you up-to-date knowing what your customers need? What assumptions are you making about your customers?

If you don't keep up with the latest purchasing trends (better known as consumer behavior), you might make incorrect assumptions or use outdated information to implement marketing strategies (more business blind spots). Here's another example about assumptions people make. This time it's about trends in the book industry. Since the introduction of Amazon's Kindle in 2007, many industry observers were quick to predict the demise of the printed book due to the emergence of the e-book. In 2014, James Surowiecki writing in *The New Yorker* said, "Some people think physical books are technologically obsolete." On the other hand, according to a recent survey by the Codex Group, "ninety-seven percent of people who read e-books say they were still wedded to print, and only three percent of frequent book buyers read only digital." Come to your own conclusion about the future of e-books.

Leaving behind the blind spots, the model of understanding customer needs is based on the belief that if you deliver a high quality product or service, at a reasonable price with a high-perceived value, you'll fulfill a need and customers will come flocking to you. Also, your existing customers will return and purchase more. Your goal is to turn customer needs into customer solutions.

Three-Step Approach to Satisfying Customer Needs

Step 1: Identify Client Need

Before I break down the model into the three steps, I'll give you a concrete example of how I worked the customer needs model with a client. I was hired by the owner of a fitness studio to put together a marketing and client retention program. This studio works with clients one-on-one in a private setting. There is no group training. Individual clients sign up for one, two, or three sessions a week.

⇆
Gather information about what your customer needs. Do not ask them for technical solutions.

This studio was losing clients faster than it was recruiting new ones. I wanted to find out what critical needs, if satisfied, would make existing clients renew their membership. From a marketing perspective, I was also interested in finding out what requirements would satisfy prospective clients and motivate them to join the studio. The information I collected would help me focus on specific strategies for creating both the marketing and client retention program.

The first thing I did was to ask each of the training staff to talk informally with existing clients. The trainers would ask just two questions to the clients:

What is one critical factor motivating you to renew your membership in our studio?

Besides the one critical factor, name one thing we do to make you happy?

After the trainers got the answers from their clients, I conducted a group session with all the trainers. Our goal was to narrow down client needs into a manageable list. The trainers listed all the needs the clients expressed. The trainers whittled down the list of client needs to include:

- **Feeling safe and not getting hurt.** During the session, clients want to feel safe and not be put in a position where they might get physically hurt.

- **Feeling special.** One-on-one fitness training requires the trainer to be knowledgeable about certain aspects of a client's life which impacts his or her fitness goals.

- **Getting a high quality workout from qualified trainers.** Clients want to know that at every session they will receive a tailor-made, high quality workout based on their fitness goals. Also, clients want to work with trainers who are experienced, credentialed, non-judgmental, warm, and welcoming.

- **Convenience and flexibility.** Clients need:

1. The studio to be open at convenient hours, and

2. To be able to easily change appointments and schedule make-up sessions.

Before we go on, let's review what we learned about understanding your customers' needs:

1. The first step is to figure out what they need. You can ask them, not from a customer satisfaction perspective, but from a need-based perspective.

2. You are searching for broad customer needs, not solutions.

3. You are also looking for what delights and makes customers happy.

4. Understanding customer need is a requirement in order to deliver a high quality product or service that has value for the customer.

Step 2: Identify the Client's Experience

Back to the fitness studio. After identifying the clients' needs based on what they told us, I then moved to the next step. Reader: don't rush through the next part or try to skip this step and jump right to figuring out solutions to meet client need.

I went back to the list of needs and for each need, I asked the trainers: "What indicators does the client use to determine if a specific need is being met?"

Let's use the first need identified by clients: the need to feel safe and not getting hurt. How does the client know he or she is safe and not in a position to get hurt?

- The client sees the studio's equipment is in tip-top condition. The client sees an uncluttered studio.

- The trainer understands each client's unique health and fitness situation.

- The trainer makes a personal connection with the client, thus building trust.

Before you go on, be sure to go through the above exercise with each need you have identified.

Step 3: Satisfy Needs

Now that the trainers had identified their clients' needs and teased out how the clients' needs are expressed and fulfilled, it was time for the trainers to generate a list of ideas to satisfy each of the clients' needs. In technical terms, the trainers were creating standard operating procedures, which were measurable.

This three-step process may seem to drag on, but you'll be rewarded when you finish. You'll have concrete, tangible, and specific strategies and tactics required to meet client needs. Pretty good.

Go back to Step 2 where you identified how client needs are expressed. We'll still use the need to feel safe and not to get hurt as an example from the fitness studio. I asked the trainers to list ideas that would satisfy the client's need to be safe and not get hurt. Initially, the trainers stumbled and suggested ideas such as "better communication," "make them feel comfortable," "have more interaction," "look out for client's well-being," "make studio neat," or "make sure client does not get hurt." Even though their suggestions were vague, it was a good start. I didn't want the trainers to feel frustrated in their attempt to satisfy their clients' needs. I worked with them to make the suggestions concrete and tangible.

I gave them one suggestion. "How about the trainers move the exercise equipment not being used out of the way? They could also make sure the mechanical arms on the functional training machine are facing up so no one will get smacked in the head." Now they got it. They understood that performing these activities would satisfy some of the needs of the clients.

Now it was the trainer's turn. They came up with other practical suggestions such as:

- Prior to starting the work-out session, the trainer tells client what to expect during the work-out.

- Trainer asks the client if he or she is experiencing any problems, which might negatively affect the workout.

- Trainer stands close to clients to spot them.

- Trainer demonstrates proper use of equipment and the right way to position client's body.

This exercise was used to address all four client needs. The result was a list of activities trainers use when working with clients. We call this list Best Practices. Now, it's your turn to make your best guess and fill out the Three Step Approach to Satisfying Customer Needs using your own business or profession.

⇆ 3-STEP APPROACH TO SATISFYING MY CUSTOMER'S NEEDS

Step 1: *Write your customer's three most important needs based on the exercise that begins on page 84:*

1. _____

2. _____

3. _____

Step 2: *For each need you identified above, list three indicators the customer uses to determine if this specific need is being met.*

Customer Need	How will your customer know this need is being met?
#1	
#2	
#3	

Step 3: *Write as many specific things you can do to meet customers' need.*

Customer Need	Tangible things you can do to meet customers' need:
#1	
#2	
#3	

Words of Wisdom

For best results in using the Three-Step Approach, consider these words of wisdom:

- Take every opportunity to get as much information as you can from your customer by asking questions.

- Never assume that you know your customer and be aware of the blind spot of making assumptions.

- Frame all your intelligence gathering in term of what problems people want to solve, not "what they need." Even though we are seeking to understand client needs, most people express their needs in terms of identifying problems.

- The only way to differentiate yourself from the competition is to satisfy unmet needs (unsolved problems).

Needs vs. Problems

Here's a quasi-fictional story. A corporation that sold laundry detergent conducted a focus group with customers who used its product. The goal was to find out how the company could improve its product. The focus group moderator was selected from the marketing department. This person had never conducted a focus group before. The facilitator asked the twelve people sitting around the conference table, "What do you need in terms of laundry detergent?" Blank stares filled the room. The participants were speechless. One participant asked, "I don't know what I need." Another said, "I need my clothes to be clean." After going in circles for a few minutes, the group was unable to articulate any need. The leader got frustrated and terminated the group after twenty minutes, without any suggestions.

The only way to differentiate yourself from the competition is to satisfy unmet needs (unsolved problems).

Another fictional company also sold laundry detergent and conducted a focus group with customers to find out how the corporation could improve its product. This time the focus group facilitator asked the right question to group members. "What problems are you having with your current laundry detergent?" The answers came rolling off everyone's tongues.

"I hate it when the liquid drips down the side of the bottle."

"I can't seem to figure out how to use the scoop."

"The directions are written too small."

"The bottle is too heavy."

"The handle is too small."

"I don't know if I'm getting my money's worth."

Let's look at how to turn problems into needs. In the left column, I listed the problems the members of the focus group had with their existing laundry detergent. In the right column, I filled in what I thought the customer needed.

⇆ TRANSLATING PROBLEMS INTO NEEDS

Customers need a quality product at the right price. The quality equation is:

quality + right price = value

Laundry detergent

I have a problem with my current laundry detergent.	What **need** must be satisfied for the purchaser to buy your product?
I don't know if I'm getting my money's worth.	I need value
I hate it when the liquid drips down the side of the bottle.	I need quality
I can't seem to figure out how to use the scoop.	I need quality
The directions are written too small.	I need quality (or reading glasses)
The bottle is too heavy.	I need quality

⇆

A good businessperson will talk about unmet needs as a way to build relationships with customers.

This was an ambitious chapter. I wanted to gently drive home the importance of knowing as much as possible about what your customer needs. I wanted you to appreciate the value of gauging customer satisfaction and understand how fleeting customer loyalty can be. The more you know about your customer, the more effective and successful your marketing strategies will be.

CHAPTER 7

Talk is Not Cheap

Before we dive into this chapter, let's review some of the communication techniques you have already learned. Reviewing these skills will make you feel good about how much you've already learned. You have created:

1. An elevator speech used when you talk with potential referral sources.

2. A power message used when talking to customers.

3. Strategies to reduce your anxiety when discussing fees.

4. A plan aimed at helping you become less apprehensive about attending networking events.

This is a great start. Good work!

I'm going to reveal secret weapons used to enhance communication between you and your customers. These are not sales gimmicks or platitudes. They are effective ways to build relationships with customers and referral sources with the goal of obtaining their business. In this chapter, you'll learn:

• The art of asking questions.

• How to fight off the urge to use jargon.

• A five step communication tool.

• How to avoid traps which destroy relationships.

Did you ask a good question today?

This is one of my favorite stories. The lesson is profound and forms the basis of the ideas presented in this chapter. Isador Rabi was a Polish-born American physicist and Nobel laureate. He was recognized in 1944 for his discovery of nuclear magnetic resonance, which is used in magnetic resonance imaging. When asked if there were any significant influences on his life, he said, "My mother made me a scientist without ever intending to. Every other Jewish mother in Brooklyn would ask her child after school: "So? Did you learn anything today?" But not my mother. "Izzy," she would ask, "did you ask a good question today?" That difference – asking good questions – made me become a scientist. (As quoted in "Great Minds Start with Questions" in *Parents Magazine,* September 1993).

Izzy got it. It's about asking questions. It's about engaging in a dialogue. As you move through this chapter, you'll be reminded of just how important it is to ask questions.

I didn't know about Isador Rabi when I started my first job after graduate school. One of the managers where I worked took me under his wing and told me two things I'll never forget.

1. During your first month or so, don't impress people with how much you know. Don't offer up solutions or suggestions. Just ask questions. Ask as many questions as you can to as many people as you can.

2. Carry a yellow pad with you at all times when you are walking around the office.

There were two reasons to always carry a yellow pad. The first was it would not look good to others for me to walk around the office empty-handed. After all, "Idle hands are the devil's workshop." I needed to appear as though I was doing something pertaining to work. The second reason was when I'd ask a question, I'd surreptitiously write down what others said. I kept this list handy and used it as a reference when I would be in a position to answer questions rather than ask questions. From this point on I never stopped asking questions.

Back to the Future

I found this amazing insight on ethics and interpersonal relationships taken from the Talmud written more than 1,900 years ago.

> A wise man does not speak before one who is greater than him in wisdom or in years; he does not interrupt the words of his fellow; he does not rush to

answer; he asks what is relevant to the subject matter and replies to the point; he speaks of first things first and of last things last; concerning that which he has not heard, he says, "I have not heard," and he acknowledges the truth.

When I first read this, I thought whoever wrote it must have been a salesman. This short paragraph summarized the most important components of building strategic relationships. For me, the first phrase *"A wise man does not speak before one who is greater than him in wisdom or in years,"* is more about wisdom than age. Think about it. If you are meeting with potential referrers or prospective customers, who have been working in their business for many years, they are going to know more about their business than you.

Many veteran business owners and managers are keepers of the oral history of their business and information about their industry or profession. Don't dismiss these business veterans as dinosaurs. You and I have plenty to learn from these folks. They are wiser in many ways. And, in order to take advantage of their wisdom, you have to learn how to listen. Yes, listen; with a capital L. It's what we're going to do in this chapter.

The second part, *"he does not interrupt the words of his fellow,"* is something which does not come easily to some people. I've always wanted to record a video of my family – my wife, my two adult children, and two of my wife's adult children – sitting around the dinner table. Everyone is talking at the same time. Interruptions are frequent. The introverted children can't seem to get a word in edgewise. To say the least, it's chaotic and frustrating for me, even though I talk a lot and interrupt. It seems like everyone has the most important thing in the world to share.

Has this ever happened to you? You're listening to a customer and at some point in the conversation, you can't wait to say something in response to what they are saying. Chances are, at some time during the conversation, you'll interrupt the other person. This conversation then devolves into two monologues – yours and theirs. And, to make things worse, in order to be heard, one of you might talk over the other.

The next phrase states, *"he does not rush to answer."* Our brain is wired to have the ability to solve complex problems. We've become so good at problem solving it comes naturally to us. Think about a time when a friend or relative came to you complaining about a work problem. Did you rush to try and the fix the problem?

Yup. Before I created the Relationship Building Strategy, I would be talking with a client about a marketing challenge and I would be saying to myself, "I've heard this problem a hundred times and I have plenty of fixes." I was rushing to answer instead of building the relationship and probing deeper to find the root cause of the problem or hearing the client's own insight to solve the problem.

The following phrase says, *"he asks what is relevant to the subject matter and replies to the point."* When you are in the midst of a dialogue with a customer or referrer, you want to keep your comments brief and to the point. You ideally want to keep the customers focused on their needs as much as you can. Remember, it's not about you! Sometimes, when I'm with a prospect, I lapse into, what my wife calls, "my strident mode." I sound like I'm dogmatic in the way I come across. When I feel myself getting stirred up, I tell myself to return to the land of listening.

"He speaks of first things first and of last things last." The goal of your initial conversations with prospects is to build a relationship. You build relationships by following the steps of the Relationship Building Strategy. You don't want to do what car salesmen used to do. When a customer walked into the car showroom, the sales man would try to hook them and start closing the sale by asking, "What color car are you looking for?" This tactic might work for selling cars. Will it work for you? I don't think so.

And finally, the phrase *"concerning that which he has not heard, he says, 'I have not heard,' and he acknowledges the truth."* Do you know how hard it is to answer a question by saying, "I don't know" or "I've never heard of this." I think I have all the answers. After all, I'm the "subject matter expert." It's okay to say, "I don't know." Will it tarnish your credibility? Nope. Will it make you more authentic? Yes. Maybe you will even learn something, too.

How to Destroy a Business Relationship in Three Easy Steps

You can learn all the best sales techniques in the world and have a great product or service to offer your customers but if you don't watch out for and address the three most common business relationship destroyers, you might as well close up shop.

⚡
Negativity begets
negativity.

Destroyer #1: Focus on negativity

Negativity shows up in us when our limbic system perceives a threat. As mentioned earlier, your thinking brain (pre-frontal cortex) goes offline, reactivity sets in, and you're left with raw emotions. This is when your flight or fight response kicks in. You can easily ruin a sale and possibly sabotage your reputation by acting like a Debbie Downer or Walter Whiner. Debbie and Walter are lost in the netherworld of negativity. Debbie and Walter are scanning for danger and hear most things from a prospective customer as negative. The opposite is also true. Everything (well, almost) that comes out of Debbie's and Walter's mouths sounds negative. The negativity can be heard in tone of voice and or in the negative messages that are communicated. The worst thing you can do is to find faults in your prospective client's opinions.

Destroyer #2: Take things personally

I had an appointment with a new client at 1 p.m. at my office. The client confirmed his appointment the day before via email. At 1 p.m. he was not there; at 1:15 p.m. he was not there. At 1:30 p.m. I called his cell phone and my call went right to voice mail. This incident happened before the advent of text messaging. I said to myself, "This guy is not coming. What did I say to him that would make him change his mind about meeting me?" I ruminated about all possible things I said to turn him off. Emotionally, I beat myself up good. So, what happened next? He arrived at 1:30 p.m. I had written down the wrong time in my calendar. I was exhausted after the session and my exhaustion was not based on what we accomplished.

Destroyer #3: Interpret what customers are saying

This destroyer rears its ugly head when you guess what the other person is thinking. Destroyer #3 occurs when you make up stories about yourself. Every one of us is guilty when it comes to interpreting customers or what anyone says. I like to say you are making up a story about the other person.

You are emotionally and financially invested in making your business succeed. You want to make the right decisions in order for your business to grow. It is easy to fall into the trap of interpreting what customers say when you feel vulnerable and nervous.

I was helping a client create his website. My role was to coordinate the project and act as a liaison between the web designer and my client. I interviewed four web designers and made my recommendation. My client agreed with my recommendation and signed a contract with the designer I'll call Alexis. Alexis' first deliverable was a rough design of how the website would look. When I saw the design, I was horrified. It looked like a fifth grader did it. My client likewise went ballistic when he saw Alexis' work.

After I saw the design, I talked to my client on the phone. I did not know what to say except to agree with him. I was at a loss for words. I unconsciously began making up stories about what happened. "Maybe Alexis did not understand the directions. Maybe she was having a bad day. Or maybe Alexis didn't want to work with us. Maybe the websites she showed me were not hers." Maybe . . . maybe . . . maybe.

My client had serious reservations about continuing to work with Alexis. However, he decided to give Alexis one more chance. On the next go-around Alexis nailed it. She captured what my client wanted. Alexis listened carefully and delivered.

The ending is a bit bizarre. The final website was more than what my client expected. He was delighted and proud to launch it. My client told me he was not interested in knowing what happened. My client thought it best just to move on. I'll never know what happened.

One more illustration of how I made up a story and, of course, the story turned out to be dead wrong. I was coaching Andy, a sole proprietor of a tax preparation and accounting service. Andy hung out his shingle one year prior to our meeting. He told me how much he appreciated the help I gave him and valued our time together. One theme we regularly discussed was how to handle his irregular cash flow. His work was seasonal and cash pretty much dried up after tax season.

Our coaching sessions were either on the phone or via Skype and held every other week. Sometimes we'd have a double session. As a coach and advisor, I generally meet with clients for a full hour. A double session would be for two hours and billed for two hours. After each session, I emailed Andy his bill.

Our first two sessions were in January. Andy paid me at the end of January for the two sessions. The same thing happened in February. In March and early April, we met twice for one hour and once for a double session. I emailed my bill after each of the March and April sessions. By late April, I had not received a check from Andy. Andy canceled his next session via email and wrote that he had to stop for a while without any explanation. Right before I received the email, I said to myself I would not see him until his bill was paid.

I wondered what was going on. Why wouldn't he pay? Why did he quit? So, I made up a story or two in my head about why Andy didn't pay. After a few days of not getting a check in the mail and after making up some stories, I decided to email Andy and attach a copy of the bill and ask him what was going on. I did not receive a reply. So, I made up more stories. "Maybe he didn't value our work?"

A week later, I called him and left a message for him to call me. I was polite and just asked him to return my call. No response. It was now the first week in May, when Andy called back. He apologized for not getting back to me. He said he was completely overwhelmed during tax season. He sent me a check the next week for the full amount.

Going from Mr. Fix-it to Mr. Listening

I was hired by the director of a group medical practice to create and implement a marketing program. The goal was to increase the number of insured patients. This seemed like a doable goal. I've done it before with good results. The first place to start a project like this is to interview the staff involved in patient care. After interviewing the physicians, staff, and the medical director, I got a clear sense of what was going on in the practice. It seems the medical director was getting pressure from his staff to increase patient volume. The medical director told me he was satisfied with the current insured patient volume but felt forced to create a marketing program.

I had three meetings with the medical director to narrow down specific marketing objectives and discuss what had to be done internally in order to create and implement a marketing program. At each meeting the same thing happened. I would make a suggestion and he would give me reasons why my suggestion would not work. This negativity and pushback was a sure-fire way to sabotage my efforts. This back and forth went on two more times until I realized the marketing effort was going to stall out. I tried one more time to get some traction on starting the marketing program. This time the medical director told me he thought we should just update their website and maybe that would help.

Now I had a decision to make. I could either talk about what was needed in order to update the website. Or I could go back and talk about implementing the marketing program. Or, I could just listen and see what happened.

This turned out to be a transformational moment for me. I decided I needed to become Mr. Listening and say goodbye to Mr. Fix-It. In other words, instead of trying to solve this medical director's problem, I decided to use my relationship building skills and focus solely on him. The next time we met, I asked him how things were going. He told me the other doctors were pushing him to get the marketing program started. I replied, "Sounds like you feel under pressure." I took what he was telling me and reflected his feelings (No, this is not a psychotherapy ploy, but an effective way to connect with someone). "Yes," he said.

The rest of the conversation consisted of me summarizing what he said, and validating what he was experiencing. I did not make one suggestion. I did not say what I thought, and I did not try to solve his problems.

At the end of our meeting, he said, "I feel like you really unjderstand my situation." The medical director looked relieved. When I returned, I told my wife, Gail what happened. She asked me what it was like for me. I said I had to bite my tongue not to blurt out solutions. We both laughed.

The story ends with me getting paid for the time I put in, but there would be no marketing program. There would be no website update. This was okay for me. I couldn't help but wonder if this was the first time anyone actually listened to the medical director.

Giving Advice vs. Listening

Here are two quick exercises for you. I'm having you do this so you can get your feet wet before we dive into the Relationship Building Strategy pool. There are no right or wrong answers.

The first exercise concerns a customer who is unsatisfied with the product or service you have provided. If you have not started your business or do not have direct contact with a customer, think of the type of customers you want and something with which they might be dissatisfied or frustrated. For this exercise, it doesn't matter whether you talk to this person on the phone or face-to-face. The customer tells you about his or her dissatisfaction or frustration.

Exercise #1:

Briefly write down the customer's dissatisfaction or frustration.

_____

_____

_____

Now write down three questions you might ask the dissatisfied customer based on what was put forth above.

1. _____

_____

2. _____

_____

3. _____

_____

The second exercise is almost the same but instead of responding to a customer's dissatisfaction, you respond to a question from the customer.

Exercise #2

In a one sentence, write down the customer's question.

_____

_____

_____

Now write down two open-ended questions you might ask. Do not ask a question that requires a "yes" or "no" answer.

1. _____

_____

2. _____

_____

What did you learn about yourself from completing the above two exercises?

Regardless of the type of service you provide or product you sell, you're doing the same thing: solving your customers' problems and responding to their needs. Remember what you learned in Chapter 6 about customer needs. It doesn't matter if you sell a low emotional involvement product (such as a garden hose) or provide a high emotional involvement service (tax preparation services), you are solving problems and listening.

Listening is a positive act: you have to put yourself out to do it.

—David Hockney

Are You a Good Listener?

What does all this listening stuff have to do with marketing your business? Plenty. One of the many ways to build and manage strategic relationships is by listening to what customers want and listening for their unmet needs. You can't hide behind your laptop, shoot off emails to customers, and expect to make a lasting personal connection. A personal connection is more about getting to know the customer as a person. It is not getting to know personal things about the customer's likes. I hesitate to say you just want to make a professional connection because it sounds too sterile and impersonal. Listening is your key to success.

It's time to assess your listening skills. Be honest with yourself. Please answer each of these questions as honestly as you can.

↰ TEST YOUR LISTENING SKILLS

Check only one box in each row.	Hardly ever	Occasionally	Sometimes	Frequently	Almost always
1. While someone is talking to you about a problem, are you thinking about how to solve it? (**solve problem**)					
2. When you are talking with someone, do you find yourself speaking at the same time? (**over talk**)					
3. Do you tune out other people if they say something you disagree with? (**tune out**)					
4. When another person is telling you about an experience they had, do you respond by talking about your own experience? (**identification**)					
5. If someone is talking about a topic that makes you uncomfortable, do you change the subject? (**change topic**)					
6. Do you feel like you have to say something to fill in a silence? (**silence**)					
7. Do you find yourself finishing other people's sentences? (**interrupt**)					
8. When you're enthusiastic about something you're selling, do you load up your conversation with lots of facts? (**too much information**)					
9. Do you feel confrontational when a person pushes back on what you're saying? (**confront**)					
10. In a conversation, do you want the other person to agree with you? (**need agreement**)					
11. Do you say negative things to your customers about your competition? (**negativity**)					
12. In a rush to make the sale, you don't ask probing questions. (**rushing**)					
Total number of checks in each row					

How many **Almost Always** did you check?

Which one of the **Almost Always** that you selected would you like to improve?

What is **one thing** you can do to improve on this?

As I have said throughout *Critical Connections,* it's always helpful to write things down. In the space below, write one thing you learned about yourself in term of listening skills after you completed the exercise above.

When it comes to listening, I am good at:

_____

_____

_____

When it comes to listening, I need to work on (see pape 101):

_____

_____

_____

I've attended many sales training programs over the years. As part of one program, each participant had to rate his or her own listening skills on a scale of 1 to 10, with 10 being very effective. Listening was defined as "the ability to know what your customer is communicating to you – both verbally and non-verbally." What does it mean? How do I know if I'm effective? How can I check out non-verbal reactions if I'm talking on the phone? None of this made sense to me.

The trainer who was conducting the program asked us to be open when someone is giving us criticism. Okay, how do I do it? What does open mean? These exercises were too thin for me and contained little substance.

All I could think of during the training program was what I had been told over the years.

"Listen to what your customer is saying."

"Use your listening skills."

We have two ears and one mouth so that we can listen twice as much as we speak.
                                                    —Epictetus, Greek stoic philosopher

Ready to learn a new way of listening? Ready to dump the term listening? It's time to learn how to build relationships.

Relationship Building Strategy in Action

Finally, here is what you've been waiting for. In order to make the Relationship Building Strategy come alive, we'll go through each of the five steps. We'll start with a customer or referral source asking you a question regarding a problem he or she is currently experiencing or stating a frustration he or she might have. For our discussion, you have already introduced yourself and have shared your elevator speech or power message.

Step 1: Be Curious

When the customer asks you a question or states a frustration, the very first thing you do is to take the question or the stated frustration, throw it back, and **ask the customer for clarification.** Just remember what Izzy Rabi's mother asked him, "Izzy, did you ask a good question today?"

⇄
Ask for a clarification.

You might say:

"What exactly do you mean?"

"Tell me more about it."

"Can you clarify your question?"

During this initial step of the relationship, do not jump into problem-solving mode (keep Mr. or Ms. Fix-It at home). Do not answer the question. If you answer the question, you're not going to get the entire picture and the context of the question. Hang back. Take a deep breath.

By not immediately answering the question, you have time to think about your response. You also shift the burden of the conversation to the other person. This process also slows down the conversation. The slowing down process is perhaps the most important tactic you have.

Why are we answering a question with a question? I know, you've been told from an early age not to answer a question with a question. It's okay not to initially answer a question when you're building a relationship. Read on to see how Step 2 will help you control the conversation.

Step 2: Ask a Question

You read it right, ask another question or two or three. You are now in serious curiosity mode. Stay in the groove for a few more questions. If you need to, use the same questions you asked in Step 1. Your questions should be in direct response to something the customer said. Do not ask a question for the sake of asking a question. Keep in mind at any time during your conversation, if you are unsure of what to say, ask a question.

> The skill of slowing down the conversation is the most effective listening tool you have.

I've been able to sustain lengthy conversations with customers just by asking questions. It doesn't matter if they are just chatting or have a problem they want me to solve. I'm focusing all my attention on them, not me.

Step 3: Get the Gist

The next step is for you to get the gist and summarize what the other person is saying. Do not minimize how powerful this is in building a relationship. You are sending a message that you're willing to hear the other person's point of view. When you summarize, you are purposefully slowing down the other person's thinking process. The process of summarizing what the other person is saying takes the burden away from you to say something or problem-solve. This is good. You are not ready to provide answers or solve problems.

You can say:

"Let me see if I got it . . ."

"Are you saying . . ."

"Let me understand this . . ."

> You can never ask enough good questions.

If the other person corrects you, then summarize again until the other person agrees with your summary.

When you have summarized well, your customer will feel you really understood him.

Step 4: Ask for a Solution

At this point in the conversation, you should have enough information to move into problem solving. The following questions are rarely asked. Here is a series of questions you can ask:

"What have you done in the past to resolve this problem?"

"Did it work?"

"Do you have any ideas or suggestions about how you might solve this problem?"

This is very important. Our customers have more insight than they know. Sometimes, the best solutions are their own. When they figure out the answer or solution, it increases their self-confidence and competence.

Step 5: Answer the Question

Now ask, "What's Your Question?" Their question might have changed as they explore their solutions. This can be used at any time during your conversation. You can deploy this weapon when your customer or referrer starts going into detail about a problem or frustration. If you feel like you are being bombarded with this person's remarks, then politely ask, "What's your question?" This secret weapon, if used tactfully, will help the other person focus on what they are looking for. Asking, "What's your question," will make it easier for them to give you more information about the situation.

Now you can finally make your own suggestion for a solution.

⇆ RELATIONSHIP BUILDING STRATEGY AT-A-GLANCE

Step 1: Ask for clarification

Step 2: Ask more questions

Step 3: Get the gist

Step 4: Ask for their solution

Step 5: Answer their question or give advice

Here Comes the Jargon Police

In Chapter 5, *In and Out of an Elevator,* you were introduced to the dreaded word "jargon." Jargon is defined as "special words or expressions used by a particular profession or group that are difficult for others to understand." Jargon is "technical talk."

Here's a quick review of what I said in Chapter 5. Keep in mind the jargon police are out there monitoring you.

In terms of your elevator speech and power message, using jargon can be a big turn-off for those listening to you. When you use jargon, there is a good chance the person listening to you might not understand what you are saying. This is not a good way to make a first impression.

Because you have a general script to use, it's easier to eliminate jargon in your elevator speech and power message than it is in extended conversations. But, when moving deeper into conversation, and when your prospect asks more probing questions, the chances of slipping into jargon are much greater.

Is there ever a time to use jargon? Here's an easy answer: it depends!

Time to Test Your Jargon Usage

Here's a chance to eliminate jargon words from your vocabulary when talking to customers. However, there might be times when you want to use jargon. When you're talking shop with a colleague or giving a presentation to your peers, using jargon and technical terms makes sense. But, it's still best to keep the use of jargon to a minimum. Take a few minutes to do the *Jargon Buster Exercise*.

Example of Jargon Used by a Management Consultant:

Here are 5 jargon words or phrases unique to an industry or business.	A non-technical common word or phrase substituted for each jargon word or phrase from the left column.
Brand equity	Name recognition that might result in increased sales
Out of the Box	Creative thinking
Above board	To be honest and open
Scope creep	A project that expands beyond it's original goal
Pain point	A critical customer need

Your Jargon Buster Exercise

List 5 jargon words or phrases that are unique to your industry, profession or business:	Take each jargon word or phrase from the left column and substitute a non-technical common word or phrase.
1.	
2.	
3.	
4.	
5.	

Three Key Relationship Building Tips

1. When you talk to customers or referrers, use their language. The best place to start is to ask a lot of questions. They will tell you what you need to know.

2. Think of a customer rejection as an opportunity. Chances are what the customer initially says is not the real issue at hand. Once again, ask questions to ferret out underlying objections. If the customer says your fee or price is out of his or her price range, come right out and acknowledge you are asking for a premium fee or price. Don't argue, just put it out there in a dispassionate manner.

3. During the course of your conversation with a customer or referrer, you might want to tell a brief happy-ending story. This is a real story, not one fabricated to impress the customer. The story should be as short as possible, probably not more than two or three minutes.

In this chapter, you learned the importance of using listening skills to build and maintain strategic relationships. You learned the value of asking questions and how to communicate without the use of jargon. And most importantly, you learned a structured approach to understanding your customers' needs, which will increase customer satisfaction and result in more business for you.

CHAPTER 8

Managing Strategic Relationships

It's finally time to explore my definition of marketing as the management of strategic relationships. We'll identify two different types of strategic relationships:

- Relationships with referrers

- Relationships with customers or clients

These are two broad types of relationships, better known as target groups. For some businesses, the difference between a customer and a referrer is blurry. Customers can be referrers and referrers can be customers. Your job is to create and implement a plan to take care of and feed your strategic relationships. In the next two chapters, we'll cover, in detail, how to implement your plan and determine which tactics to use. In the meantime, it's all about relationships, not tactics.

⇄ *In this chapter, we are answering the question, **who** are our customers and referrers. Do not jump ahead and think about **what methods** you're going to use to get customers. Another way to say this is **think target, not tactic.***

What do I mean by managing strategic relationships. First, let's break down this definition of marketing.

- **Management.** I use the term management to describe any activity you do to keep your marketing engine running. I think of management as the art of making lists. Whether you're self-employed or own a small business, there are certain planning activities you have to do prior to initiating and maintaining relationships. This includes everything from compiling names for a newsletter to putting together timelines for the distribution of promotional informa-

↺ *Management is the art of making lists.*

tion (online or in print). I want to remind you I'm excluding information about how to reach your target markets.

- **Strategic.** I think of the word strategic as describing something important and vital. Certain relationships are vital and others are not. As we move through the book, you'll be identifying those relationships you consider strategic.

- **Relationships.** I earlier mentioned that customer loyalty is waning. If you want to keep customers, you must build and maintain relationships. There are two goals involved in building and maintaining relationships. One is to get the customer or client to purchase your service or product. And, two is to delight customers or clients so much that they will return.

Strategic Relationships with Referral Sources

Follow this two-step process as you begin to identify potential referral sources.

Step 1: Drill Down to Identify Referral Sources

Let's start with managing strategic relationships with existing and potential referrers. Remember Nicole? She wanted to start a math tutoring service for high school students. She identified high schools as a primary referral source for her business. She did her research and found there were 46 high schools in surrounding towns. This sounds like a great market for her services. Sounds good in theory but in reality, how do you build a relationship with a high school? You don't.

You can answer the above question by drilling down and seeing what happens. Identifying high schools is a good place to start. Nicole's client is not the high school student in need of tutoring. It is the person at the school who will contact the parent. When asked to drill down to identify those in a good position to refer, Nicole discovered a treasure trove of referral sources all within the walls of a high school. She was immediately able to identify high school guidance counselors, math department heads, math teachers, the parent-teacher association, and, of course, the child's parent. The head of the math department finds out about Nicole's services, contacts the student's parents, and recommends Nicole. However, Nicole cannot stop with building strategic relationships in the high school.

With my help and input from workshop participants, she was able to identify other referral sources such as psychologists in private practice and private educational testing services. The referral is made; the child is helped and gets great scores on the SAT. Everyone is happy.

Drill Down Deeper – Find individual names

Meet Jason, an occupational therapist in solo practice. He wants to promote his rehabilitative services to the clients of personal injury lawyers. Here's what he did.

Jason decided to contact the local and state bar associations, and see if they rent their mailing list of lawyers who specialize in personal injury. He looked for other resources: the good old Yellow Pages phone book and online directories of specialty membership organizations for personal injury lawyers. He found the names of gatekeepers. Gatekeepers keep vendors at bay, restricting access to the lawyers. He even went to the public library. The library has all sorts of business directories.

Step 2: Determine Your Service Area

Let's see how Jason drilled down to identify potential referrers using a demographic approach.

Jason determined that his service area would encompass office buildings located near the municipal and district courts in his county. He knew that most of the personal injury lawyers had their offices nearby. He expanded his service area to a five-mile radius from the municipal and district courts, to make sure he was covering sufficient territory. These determinations were based on such factors as:

- Is it convenient for the referrer to meet in person?
- Are there large concentrations of referrers in one area?
- Is it convenient for potential clients?

The List

Now it's your turn. Write the names of as many types of referral sources as you can. Take your time doing this. I find if you bounce your ideas off another person, you'll probably come up with at least one type of referrer you have not included. Some people call it brainstorming. I call it a good thing to do.

Types of Referrers

1. _____
2. _____
3. _____
4. _____
5. _____
6. _____
7. _____
8. _____
9. _____
10. _____

Are you satisfied that this list includes the right type of referrers you need to drive your business forward? If you are happy with this list, move ahead.

Primary or Secondary Referrers?

Now take the types of referrers you listed above and decide whether they are primary or secondary referrers. Think of primary referrers as those vital few referrers who send you the bulk of your business. Think of secondary referrers as potential sources of referrals.

In the table below, you can see some of the characteristics of referrers.

Who Are Primary and Secondary Referrers?

Primary Referrer	Secondary Referrer
Sends the most customers to you	Has the potential to send customers to you
Generates most of your revenue	Doesn't generate as much revenue
Has contact with you or knew of you in the past	Has little or no previous knowledge of you or your business
Might have some current professional connection with your business	Does not have direct connection to your business
	Might find your business online
Needs little education about your business	Needs to be educated about your business
Small number of referrers	Large number of potential referrers

Now go back to your list of referrers and determine whether they are primary or secondary, based on the characteristics listed in the table above. Put a check mark under Primary or Secondary.

Name of Referral Source	Primary	Secondary

If your business is primarily referral-based, this should have been an easy exercise. If your primary strategic relationship is with customers, please read on.

Strategic Relationships with Customers or Clients

In my marketing workshops, I always ask participants, "Who are your customers?" In some cases, the answer is "the public." I hear this from a range of people from personal coaches to those selling exotic teas. Then, someone will say, "Everyone needs my product or service." Whoa! Slow down.

In the United States, the public consists of 320 million people, excluding cats and dogs. Let's try this again. "Who are your customers?"

An esthetician might say her clients are women between the ages of 35 and 50 who have acne. Nicole's customers are parents of high school math students. The customers of the owner of a shoe store specializing in selling shoes and orthotics are those who have foot problems and have a hard time finding comfortable shoes. The craftsman who creates specialty items for Jewish weddings would consider his customers to be engaged Jewish couples.

I have two broad categories of customers:

1. Individuals who are in the process of building a business and are interested in:
   a. Marketing workshops
   b. One-on-one coaching
2. Small businesses who want:
   a. Strategic marketing consulting
   b. Organizational development training

My primary customers are individuals in the process of building their business and my secondary customers are small businesses.

Take a few minutes to think about your customers. Write down three customer categories and determine whether they are primary or secondary.

Customer Category	Primary	Secondary

If you are having a hard time narrowing down your customers, allow yourself to "get it roughly right." John Maynard Keynes is reported to have said, "It is better to be roughly right than precisely wrong."

Referral and Customer Tracking – The Big Picture

Once you identify your customers and referrers, you need to find a way to prioritize and categorize them. I use a three-tiered model to track customer sales and their purchasing patterns. I call the top tier the *Vital Few*. The Vital Few (from the *Pareto principle*) are top customers or referrers who generate the most revenue. I equate revenue generation with loyalty. I call the middle tier the *Middle Majority* and the bottom tier the *Forget-About-Ems*.

Some marketing experts use the 80/20 rule, or Pareto principle, to analyze revenue generated by customers. This rule states that a small group of customers – approximately 20 percent – produce about 80 percent of your revenue. There are statistical methods to determine this, but for the sake of using the *Critical Connections* approach, we'll call top revenue generators the Vital Few. These are your most loyal customers or clients; loyal customers will purchase more and spend more money than anyone in the other two groups.

Customer Retention

From a business perspective, your strategy is to retain the Vital Few group as top-tier customers. Your top customers expect to be rewarded and treated special. How? Think of some type of non-gimmicky type of retention program. Look at what your competition is doing. What ideas can you think of from other businesses or professions? Key point: think customer retention.

There is a thin line between customer retention and marketing. Both fit the definition of marketing as the management of strategic relationships. It's okay to blur the lines, as long as you know it. If you feel overwhelmed by the idea of starting a customer retention program, put it on your back burner.

Now it's time to think about some tangible and concrete ideas you might have for a customer retention program. What can you do on an on-going basis to keep your customers engaged? For example, I offer discounted fees for one-on-one coaching if someone attends one of my marketing workshops. When someone signs up for coaching, I add the person to my Vital Few list. Now, as being one of a select Vital Few, they qualify for further discounts on workshops, master classes, and other marketing services I offer. In addition, I occasionally send them special white papers I write on marketing or other content-related information.

Time out

I know we are in the midst of discussing the most important aspect of marketing – your customers and referrers. Why did I suddenly shift gears and talk tactics? This goes against everything I've said so far. What's up? There comes a time in the discussion of strategic relationships, when you might come up with ideas to retain customers and referrers. I don't want you to hold this idea in your head until you read the next two chapters of *Critical Connections*. It's okay to deviate from the path. Who knows where you might wind up?

List five things you can do to reward your top-tier Vital Few customers.

1. _____

2. _____

3. _____

4. _____

5. _____

Back to the Middle Majority and the Forget-About-Ems. The bulk of your customers will fall into the second tier from the top – the Middle Majority. When you think of what to do with the Middle Majority, ask yourself the following two questions.

What's one thing I can do to push Middle Majority customers up a tier to the Vital Few list?

_____

_____

What's one thing I can do to prevent the Middle Majority from slipping down a tier to the Forget-About-Ems?

_____

_____

The bottom tier is called the Forget-About-Ems. This group generates the least amount of business. Sometimes they drop off the face of the earth. These are sporadic or one-time customers or referrers. The chances of them moving up to the Middle Majority are slim to none. If I sound skeptical, it is because I've spent too much time and effort courting their business.

A word or two about *splitters*. Splitters are on-again off-again purchasers. They have no loyalty to you. This group is different from the Forget-About-Ems because splitters do purchase, albeit occasionally. This is an elusive group and it is hard to gain their loyalty. Just be aware of splitters and don't lose sleep over them.

If you have positive experiences with 99 out of 100 customers, you might ruminate about the one customer who had a bad experience with you and your business. Forget-About-Em.

Getting Organized

My friend, Deb Shaver owns her own company called Lifestyle Solutions. According to her website, Lifestyle Solutions is dedicated to managing the business of living by organizing people, money, places, and things. Deb is a professional organizer. She's been in business for more than fifteen years. Deb originally worked her business by herself and currently employs four staff.

Deb's successful marketing story is by no means earth shattering or innovative. At the beginning of her career, Deb knew she could not launch her business without some guidance. She worked with a mentor for more than year. Her mentor was a seasoned professional organizer and board member of a professional organizer's association.

In her first two years, Deb's primary referral source was her mentor. Having a mentor provided Deb with the direction and insight needed to start and promote a personal services business.

Deb had a strong strategic relationship with her mentor. When she first started her business, she did not have a specific target group in mind. She just wanted clients. Or put another way, she did not think in terms of what type of person would make an ideal client. What she did have was time to learn.

In the beginning she put ads in the Yellow Pages, attended networking events, and placed flyers in local churches, synagogues, and most any public bulletin board she could find. Deb got her first client from an advertisement she ran in the Yellow Pages. In fact, Deb retained this client for five years after the initial project was complete.

Some other successful relationships for Deb came through her becoming an active member in two membership associations for professional organizers. At one association, Deb was elected to be on the executive board. In this capacity, she organized an internal networking group. Over a five-year period, Deb targeted her referral marketing efforts to banks and investment firms that represented clients who wanted help in tracking their income, expenses, and assets. Deb would build strategic relationships with the bank or investment firm's advisors. The advisors slowly started referring their clients to Deb.

The Style Editor of *Washingtonian Magazine* contacted Deb's professional association looking for a professional organizer to interview for a feature story. Deb was featured twice in the *Washingtonian Magazine*. Because of these articles, she got more referrals.

Deb tried using auctions at local schools and religious organizations as a way to promote her business. No luck, not even a phone call.

During the first few years of being in business, Deb created a talk entitled "Life Is a Network." She would present her talk to students and professional groups. Deb knew this was not going to be a way for her to get more business. She just wanted to share her experiences with others, especially young professionals just starting out in their careers. When Deb's business started growing, she did not have the time to pursue speaking engagements.

At the same time that Deb's business started to grow, she noticed her existing clients referred most of her new clients. Clients were happy with Deb's service and referred their friends. Deb's main marketing strategy was actually no strategy at all. She took advantage of word-of-mouth. Or, in my vernacular, Deb leveraged strategic relationships with both potential clients and referral sources.

As the digital era came to life, Deb still relied on tried and true efforts to build her business:

- Word-of-mouth

- Repeat business from existing customers

- Solid professional relationships with referrers

- Active involvement in professional associations

She doesn't tweet. She doesn't post on Facebook, She doesn't blog. But, her business grows. Go figure.

Strategic Relationships: A Personal Story

Over the years, my wife Gail has heard me go on and on, pontificating about my definition of marketing as the management of strategic relationships. She would politely listen and then move on and talk about something not related to marketing.

A few years ago, I broached the idea of conducting workshops for psychotherapists on building a private psychotherapy practice. Gail was enthusiastic and we developed a curriculum.

From being in practice for more than 30 years, Gail knew that psychotherapists don't feel comfortable "marketing their practice." Some feel marketing is not ethical. Some confuse marketing with advertising (print, broadcast, or online) and don't feel qualified to be a marketer.

During the first workshop, I presented the marketing as the management of strategic relationships concept. Gail told me she was struggling with understanding this concept, even though she had heard me talk about it in the past year. Half way through the first workshop, Gail had one of those ah-ha moments. After the workshop, she told me that while I was explaining the concept in depth, she "got it." Here's what she said. "As a psychotherapist, it's my job to build a relationship with my client. That's what psychotherapists do." The business of psychotherapy is one of connecting in a relationship. The idea of marketing as the management of strategic relationships demystified the idea of psychotherapists marketing their practice.

Gail told me there are more than 148 different types of psychotherapy practiced by therapists. A number of research studies on effectiveness of different methods of psychotherapy concluded it doesn't matter what kind of therapy is done. It's the relationship between the client and therapist that matters. In fact, it's the client's perception of the quality of the relationship that matters most. It's not about what type of therapy is practiced.

So, once again, what does this have to do with marketing? No matter how you look at it, marketing is still the management of strategic relationships.

Mark B.

Mark B. owns a company that provides a service and sells a product. Mark likes to say his company is in the business of "designing and supplying house interiors, which increase new home sales." He sees his business as a way to help homeowners sell their home or builders to sell new homes.

Prior to starting his company, Mark worked for a furniture rental company, first as the comptroller. He then moved into sales, and then became executive vice-president. When his company was sold, Mark needed to find work. He secured funding and started a company focused solely on furnishing interiors to model homes.

Today, his company sells and leases furniture. His success is due, in part, to his relentless quest to create and maintain strategic relationships.

Here's a summary of Mark's marketing activities.

- His first customer was as a result of making a cold call.

- He regularly attended meetings of the local home builder's association.

- He focused on building and maintaining strategic relationships (my words) with existing customers and key referrers, such as mid-size building contractors.

- His most effective marketing strategy was word-of-mouth referrals from existing customers.

- Due to the high staff turnover in his referrers's offices, Mark resorted to other promotional tactics such as publishing a monthly newsletter, conducting educational seminars for referrers, and attending and exhibiting at trade shows. He was able to keep his print advertising costs low by using the aforementioned promotional tactics.

- Today, most of his marketing efforts are driven by social media. His social media goal is to continue to build awareness and maintain credibility. He uses Facebook, his business website, a blog, and Pinterest.

Here's what he didn't do:

- He did not volunteer to be on committees at the homebuilders association.

- He did not do any print or broadcast advertising.

- He never had a marketing person on staff.

Mark knows the value of establishing and maintaining strategic relationships. When the residential housing market took a sharp decline, Mark knew he had to make a greater effort to keep in contact with his referrers. This was hard because so many of his clients were laying off staff who were Mark's contacts. Mark persevered and slowly gained new referrers.

Hidden Strategic Relationships

Now that you have identified key strategic customer and referrer relationships, it's time to uncover some hidden ones. Think in terms of other types of people who can be a resource for you. For example, I never thought of my web designer as a strategic relationship. He has turned out to be a valuable resource for me. I've told you about my fitness center client. I originally went to the fitness center as a client, to get in shape and become healthier. I never dreamed it would become such a rewarding client. I never dreamed the owner of the fitness center would refer me to four other fitness centers based on the work I did.

Think of people you meet on a daily basis who have nothing to do with your business. Is there an opportunity to connect? List up to five hidden strategic relationships (referrer or customer):

1. _____

2. _____

3. _____

4. _____

5. _____

You're all set to jump into the land of tactics and tools. You know how to drill down to obtain the most accurate list of referrers and customers. You generated some ideas on how to retain customers. And most importantly, you identified specific primary and secondary strategic relationships.

Now that you understand how important it is to build strategic relationships with potential referrers and customers, it's time to talk about how we're going to reach them. Don't lose sight of your goal of building relationships by getting lost in the tactics.

CHAPTER 9

Tools of the Trade 1: Traditional Methods

Traditional marketing tactics remain tried and true and are the stalwarts of many large and small businesses. I find that young marketers downplay the importance of traditional marketing tactics. No matter what your age or level of marketing experience, traditional marketing tactics cannot be ignored.

Before we launch into a discussion of traditional marketing tactics, let's take a look at three fatal marketing mistakes often made by novice marketers.

Fatal Marketing Mistake #1: Starting with Tactics

I was hired by a professional membership association to develop a marketing plan. This project fell under the auspices of the association's newly formed Marketing Committee, with whom I'd be working. The members of the committee had input into all aspects of the project. At the start of the project one committee member suggested they write an informational booklet describing all the good things the association had done in the past.

The committee began to figure out what the booklet should contain. One concern was expressed about being careful to assure that the booklet should not, in any way, offend any member of the association. Suddenly, the conversation shifted from the general idea of producing a booklet to the political ramifications if the booklet were published.

The committee members liked the idea of a booklet. I asked, "Who's this booklet for?" The committee members suggested the booklet could be used to help recruit new members and educate the public. The booklet could also be used as part of lobbying efforts to educate members of Congress on key issues.

I've seen this scenario played out many times in all sorts of organizations. Someone says, "We need a brochure." Another says, "We need to send out a press release about what we're doing." Yet another says, "Let's run an ad in the local newspaper." In the case above, the Marketing Committee became fixated on "the booklet." Fatal Marketing Mistake #1 just reared its ugly head. The idea of a booklet came first, and then they tried to figure out who would be its target audience.

Now you have one booklet that has to address the unique needs of:

- Prospective members
- The public
- Lawmakers
- Members of the Marketing Committee
- The leadership of the association (after all, the leadership has to approve the budget for the production and distribution of the booklet).

How are the needs of each of these groups going to be satisfied with one booklet?

I am a strong believer in using visual cues to help me get through the day and to help me remember things I need to do. Here's one way to prevent yourself from making Marketing Mistake #1. On a 5×8 card, in black magic marker, write the following: "I will think of my customer's need first, then decide on which tactic to use."

Let me reiterate, don't think about specific tools or tactics before you consider the strategic relationship you want to build.

Fatal Marketing Mistake #2: Spreading Yourself Too Thin

A few years ago, Jackie came to me for coaching. She wanted to start a seminar business teaching communication skills to pre-marital couples. Her husband, a counseling psychologist, would conduct the seminars. Jackie would do all of the administrative work including the marketing. Jackie was passionate about her new business and couldn't wait for our first coaching session.

At our first session, we worked on creating her vision, identifying her strengths and challenges, and started working on her elevator speech and power message. From the looks of things, Jackie's business would be driven primarily by referrals. I asked Jackie to think of three important strategic relationships she could build and ways to reach out to them.

Jackie came back the next week and told me she identified clergy, the public, and marriage counselors. We decided the clergy would be the first group to tackle. Pre-marital couples sometimes meet with their minister, priest, or rabbi for counseling. These clergy are in a perfect position to refer couples to a pre-marital educational seminar. It makes sense to build relationships with clergy. So far, so good.

Then we talked about which tools of the trade Jackie could use to reach out to the clergy. As you can see below, Jackie's first tactic was to mail brochures to the clergy announcing the seminar dates. I asked her a series of questions about the logistics of getting the brochure in the hands of the right person.

Jackie suggested:	I replied:
Mail brochures announcing the seminar dates.	• What geographic region do you want to reach? • How are you going to determine how many brochures to print? • How are you going to find the names, addresses, and email addresses of the clergy? • Are there any denominations you want to exclude? If so, why? • Who is going to write, design, print, and distribute the brochure? • Can you estimate the design, printing, and postage costs? • How many times are you going to mail this brochure to this group? • Will the brochure contain time-limited information? How many seminar dates will you list?

I wanted to drill down into the details so Jackie could get a sense of what would be in store for her. She got flustered while I was asking her the questions listed above. I could imagine her limbic system getting triggered.

After asking Jackie to take a few deep breaths, we continued. Jackie thought it would be a good idea to make personal visits to clergy. I said to myself, "Good idea, but hard to do." In any case, we were off to a good start by getting Jackie to think about the details.

Jackie suggested:	I replied:
Make personal visits to clergy	• What's the goal of your visit?
	• How will you determine whom to visit?
	• What are the chances of actually getting past the gatekeeper so you can meet with the clergy person?
	• How much time during your day can you devote to this activity?

Now here's where Jackie began to spread herself too thin. So far, she identified one group – clergy – as a strategic relationship. She identified two tactics to use to build those relationships. When she began to think about what it would take to implement the two tactics (mailing brochures and making personal visits), her anxiety level skyrocketed.

Next, she suggested building a website and writing a blog. Instead of giving her my opinion, I wanted her to come up with the answers. So I started asking the hard questions. Jackie went from flustered to panic.

Jackie suggested:	I replied:
Build a website	• How much money do you want to spend?
	• Do you have a compelling domain name?
	• What do you want the website to communicate?
	• Who will write and design the website?
	• Who will update the website?
	• Will the website have the functionality of accepting registration and payment?
	• How long do you think it will take to go from concept to launch?
	• Do you want to use stock photos and graphics or use original photos and graphics?

The final blow came when Jackie suggested that she could offer a free seminar to marriage counselors. Her thought was to give these counselors a flavor of what the pre-marital communication skills workshops were like. The end goal would be to have these marriage counselors refer their clients to the seminars.

Let's stop right here and see what just happened.

This is important, so hang in there. In her highly triggered state, Jackie completely lost sight of the big picture. We were talking about creating tactics to build relationships with clergy. All of a sudden, the idea of conducting a seminar for marriage counselors popped into her mind. Jackie got derailed. This phenomenon is more common than you think.

We decided to stop at this point and re-direct our energy back to the topic at hand – building relationships with clergy. So far, Jackie had agreed to:

1. create and mail a brochure or flyer,

2. make personal visits to clergy, and,

3. start to build a website.

Jackie said these tasks were manageable.

These tactics involve many sub-tasks that have to be accomplished over time. For Jackie not to be overwhelmed, she had to figure out how to prioritize them. More on this in Chapter 13.

Fatal Marketing Mistake #3: Once is Enough

"I don't understand why no one answered my blast email marketing campaign."

"I spent all this money on mailing my brochure and no one responded."

"I ran a Facebook ad for two weeks on their News Feed, but no response."

What's up here?

Does this sound familiar? How many times should you mail or email your promotion to generate a response? We can learn a lot from the magazine publishing industry.

In order to keep subscribers from dropping their subscriptions, some magazines mail or email up to seven different renewal reminder notices. Why do they spend all this time and money on a series of mailing? Because it works for them. It might not work for you, but you get the point. In this case, more is better.

You'll hear good-meaning people say you need to mail or email 5, 10, or 15 times. There is no magic number or magic formula. You have to find what works for you.

I asked to be put on the list to receive promotional emails from a major clothing retailer. In one month, I received eleven emails from them. I was not irritated by the amount of emails I received because:

- I like their products.
- I look for special discounts and other promotions.
- If I'm not interested, it will only take two seconds to delete the email from my inbox.
- And, as a past buyer, I'll probably buy something in the future.

If you are fed up with all those emails, you can simply hit the UNSUBCRIBE link at the bottom of the email and in no time you're off the list.

It is not Fatal Marketing Mistake #3 to use multiple tactics to reach the same target group. For example, I'm going to conduct a marketing strategies workshop for women-owned business owners. I have to use:

- Email promotion – at least four different times over a 3-month period
- Online space advertising – placed three months prior to workshop
- Online directory listings – at least six months prior to workshop
- Print advertising in local and targeted business publications for at least three months
- My website – as soon as possible
- Twitter – tweet once a week for a month using content

You've heard the trite expression, "Vote early and vote often." Actually, it's not far from the truth when it comes to avoiding Marketing Mistake #3. Get your promotion out early. Keep your customer involved as often as possible by using multiple promotional vehicles. Whether you are selling a product or providing a personal or professional service, keep your marketing engine running at full throttle all the time.

Load Up Your Toolkit

Reader Beware

Tread lightly; you don't want to fall into the rabbit hole of marketing minutiae. Once you're there, you'll have a tough time climbing back up to the Land of Strategy. Living in the Land of Strategy is about – you guessed it – satisfying the needs of strategic relationships.

Critical Connections is not a compendium of how-to-do-it resources. It's not a book for dummies. If you are interested in learning about search engine optimization, or how to build a website, or to how to maximize your visibility on Facebook, go online or go to your local bookstore. I'm not saying this type of information is not important. What I am saying is for now, in the embryonic stage of your marketing plan, focus on strategic issues. You've already asked and answered some strategic questions such as:

- What is my vision for my business?
- What are my strengths and challenges involved in building my business?
- How do I overcome my fears?
- What do I say to potential referrers and potential customers?
- What are my customers' needs?
- How do I keep clients engaged?
- Who are my strategic relationships?

You've been on an exciting journey reading *Critical Connections* and it only gets better. You're going to load your toolkit with all sorts of tools and tactics to help you build and maintain strategic relationships.

Throughout this book, I've been mentioning some tools of the trade used to promote any business. I divide tools of the trade into two main groups: Traditional and electronic. If your parents were old-school marketers, they'd be familiar with traditional tools. If you're a Millennial, you'll want to keep on reading. After all, shouldn't you be keeping up with the Baby Boomers? For the rest of this chapter, we'll focus on strategic issues involved in the use of traditional tools. I'll be asking you more tough questions about the use of these tools.

Traditional marketing tools and tactics can be broken down into three general categories:

- **Written communication** can range from brochures to thank you notes.
- **In-person** tools run the gamut form presenting talks at seminars to taking a referrer to lunch.
- **Broadcast** refers to advertising on television and radio.

Old-School Brochures

At one time or another, you've probably had to write and possibly design a brochure. The brochure would have been mailed along with a cover letter to prospective customers and referrers. Even if you're a fan of email and have had past success with blast email campaigns, snail mail might be an effective vehicle to get your message across. I know from experience there are certain segments of customers who respond to snail mail.

Physicians in private practice are a good example. Many physicians use Gmail and Yahoo accounts. They generally do not check their email during the day. You may be addicted to email and check it all day. Not the case with many physicians. When in doubt, use snail mail for physicians.

Before you fire up your computer and start writing a brochure, look at the strategic relationships you listed in the previous chapter. Are any of these strategic relationships good candidates to receive a brochure in the mail? Do you know the purchasing patterns of any of your strategic relationships? Take an educated guess.

When you mail a brochure, consider the following:

- Narrow your list, so your mailing tasks will be manageable.
- Where will you get the proper mailing list? How much will the mailing list cost? Most mailing list brokers and some membership organizations will rent you their list for a one-time use. Any responses you receive from your mailing are yours to keep in your database. Make sure you shop competitively for lists.
- How many brochures and cover letters should you print? Always mail a brochure along with a cover letter unless you are printing a self-mailer.
- Who will write, design and print the brochure?
- How much will it cost for design, printing, and postage?
- Do you want to use an envelope in addition to the brochure or do you want the brochure to be a self-mailer? A self-mailer can be a large post-card or trifold.
- How much of your time will this project take?

Go online and search for direct marketing. You will find tips on how to write brochures. You will get a feeling of the range of fees and costs involved in printing and mailing a brochure.

I once heard a marketing professional say the purpose of a brochure was to be put in a filing cabinet or desk drawer. This pessimistic statement does have some merit. But let's face it, you have to have something tangible to mail and give customers.

My favorite adaptation of the brochure is what I call a capabilities sheet (some refer to it as a pitch sheet). These are printed on one side of a piece of paper only – I print mine on my color laser printer. I like them because I can change the copy to fit the specific needs of a client or referrer.

For example, I met with a lawyer in a mid-sized law firm to discuss conducting a client retention program. I had previously written a one-page capability sheet for another type of client. This particular client owned a company that provided continuing education programs for healthcare professionals. I wrote a capabilities sheet for this company to deliver a customer service training program for his twelve employees. It was easy for me to modify the existing capabilities sheet for the lawyers.

A local real estate agent in my neighborhood mails 5×8 cards to selected zip codes. The card lists all of the homes sold in the past two months, including asking and close price, specific street address, and other information. On the other side of the card she writes a "Dear Neighbor" letter describing current trends in real estate which have an impact on the local market. She also mails postcards listing houses for sale in my neighborhood.

Three tips to think about when you sit down to write a capabilities sheet:

- 1. Use bullets in the middle of the sheet.

- 2. Don't squeeze your phone number, email address, and website on the very bottom of the sheet.

- 3. Next time you check your snail mail, see if there are any postcard styles that would work with your customers or referrers.

Let Your Fingers Do The Walking

Yellow Pages are still used by consumers. For some advertisers, the Yellow Pages are a reliable source of referrals. Entrepreneur.com reports that the cost of a Yellow Page display ad varies from city to city. In New York City, a one-inch space listing costs around $2,500, and for a full-page display ad, up to $92,000. A one-inch space listing in Manhattan, Kansas, costs about $252, and $11,000 for a full-page display ad. Do you really need a display ad or is a line listing enough? Yellow Pages offer free line listings, but charge for display advertisements.

Look at the hidden cost of placing the advertisement. For example: What size do you want? Under how many categories do you want to be listed? If you place your ad through a third-party broker, there will be extra fees involved.

Newspapers & Magazines

According to a recent *Annual Report on American Journalism,* newspaper print advertising revenue is now just 45 percent of what it was in 2006. According to the Pew Research Center ". . . 55 percent of regular *New York Times* readers say they read the paper mostly on a computer or mobile device, as do 48 percent of regular *USA Today* and 44 percent of *Wall Street Journal* readers."

Costs of advertising vary greatly across the United States. Is the cost worth it based on what you read above? Do you want to advertise in national, regional, or local newspapers or magazines?

In terms of costs, you pay to have the display ad designed and you have to pay for the actual placement of the ad. How many times do you want to run the ad? Think carefully about what your goal is in placing an ad in a printed publication.

Newspaper & Magazine Coupons (paper and digital)

Coupons work for those of you selling a product or a personal service such as gutter cleaning. Some people say using coupons for a discount on professional services devalues your service. The jury is out on this. Businesses do get phone calls and email replies from customers seeing and using coupons.

What type of offer do you want to promote?

- percent discount off full price or on next purchase
- Specific dollar amount discount
- Buy one get one free
- Freebie

Also, consider co-op coupon advertising companies that place discount coupons in envelopes and mail to targeted geographic areas.

Is a coupon appropriate for your business? Which publications will you use? How many times do you want to have the coupon appear? Do you have the budget? Ask other businesses who use coupons if it is effective.

With the advent of digital coupons, including Living Social and Groupon, the use of printed coupons is decreasing. Don't be shy; explore the viability of using digital coupons. If you want to explore how to use online coupons as a tool, consult the web.

Thank You Very Much & Happy Holidays

When someone refers a customer to you, it's a good idea to send the referrer a thank you note. Think of a thank you note as another opportunity to get your name in front of a referrer. Hand written thank you notes to referrers require little effort. Don't write a long-winded tome. Be brief and to the point. Be sensitive to the age of the person who is receiving the thank you note. Don't be old-school and snail mail a thank you note to a Millennial. Use email. On the other hand, do you think sending a hand-written thank you note to Baby Boomers is appropriate? It depends. Just remember, "know your customer." Know which type of communication vehicle your customers prefer.

How many holiday cards do you receive each year between Thanksgiving and New Year? Would you be offending a Jewish or Muslim person by sending them a Christmas card? Is it worth your time to mail holiday cards? It seems like there are more questions about sending holiday cards than there are answers. If you do send holiday cards, consider wishing a Happy Thanksgiving, then there will be no religious inferences. Be sure to thank the receivers for their business during the past year.

What Business are You Really In?

When clients ask me whether they should write a newsletter (online or print), I respond by saying, "Are you in the publishing business?" Most of the time, I'll hear back, "No, but . . ." Then I ask, "What's your goal; why are you writing a newsletter? How much time, energy, and money do you want to spend doing this? If you won't write it, then who will? Will the person writing the newsletter have working knowledge of your business or industry. Will you print the newsletter or publish somewhere online, or both? How often do you want to publish it?"

One way to circumvent the potential newsletter quagmire is to blog. We'll talk about blogging in the next chapter.

Write a Letter to the Editor

If you are passionate about a local social, political, or cultural issue and this issue in some way affects your business and your customers, then consider writing a short letter to the editor. Writing letters to the editor is an easy way to reach the public.

Think carefully about what type of magazine or newspaper would publish your letter.

Have low expectations that this will bring you business, and have a lower expectation the letter will be published. The shelf life of your printed letter might be a few days. The good news is the newspaper or magazine, which publishes your letter, will probably have an online version. Your letter will be cached somewhere on the internet.

It's Time for a Commercial

Have you seriously thought about advertising on television or radio? This can be a costly endeavor. Who is going to write, produce, and place the ad for you? How much do you think this will cost? Is it worth your time? Is this a cost-effective way to reach your target audience?

The rates for airing a 30-second radio commercial in different cities range from $54 to $1,400. There are more than fifty different radio formats ranging from adult contemporary to soul music. And, there are more than fifteen talk radio formats.

You can pay anywhere from $1,000 to $3,000 for a 60-second ad on local TV. Of course, rates vary based on time of day (prime time costs more), day of week, or time of year.

You're the Expert . . . and Don't Forget It

Local radio stations, television stations, and newspapers are in need of experts. No matter what your business is, these media want to talk to you. My client, the owner of a fitness center, is interviewed on radio every January to discuss tips on how to start an exercise program. Remember the real estate agent I mentioned above? She is interviewed at least three times a year and shares insights on the state of the local real estate market. Put your stake in the ground and be the expert.

How do you get to be interviewed as the expert? Send a press release to the lifestyle or business editor of your local TV, radio, or newspaper. Your press release must address a current business topic of interest to readers, viewers, and listeners. Press releases are by no means free advertisements. Pitching business is not the goal. Editors are not interested in knowing you just started a new business. Unless, your business is totally unique and no one else in your community is providing this product or service, stick to a topic and convince the editor of your expertise.

Person-to-Person

By now, you should have sketched out your networking plan. Remember to go with your strengths and acknowledge your challenges. Join a local small business association. However, it's not worth joining local business organizations unless you volunteer to do something. Just joining is a waste of your time and money. It's no surprise that I joined a local small business association and volunteered to be on the marketing committee. By volunteering to be on a committee, I was able to get instant credibility and access to the leaders of the organization.

You can connect with business networking groups. They come in different sizes and shapes. There are business groups who charge a monthly fee; in some cities these types of groups can charge up to $500 a month. Some business groups focus only on lead generation.

We talked about networking strategies for introverts in Chapter 4. Whether you're an introvert or extrovert, it's a good idea to remind yourself of the value of attending these types of events.

Hand Me the Microphone

If you can handle the pressure of speaking in public, consider presenting a talk at local business, civic, social, community or religious organizations. You can find organizations which sponsor Lunch & Learn events, Power Breakfasts, etc. You're the subject matter expert. You have knowledge and inside information about your industry or profession, which other businesses and consumers want to know. Tailor your talk to the specific interests of the audience. Keep in mind your talk is not a sales pitch in disguise.

If you're interested in presenting a talk at a seminar or speaking at a tele-seminar and can't think of a specific topic or only have a kernel of an idea, try using this three step approach to help formulate your thinking.

✓ **Write it Down**

✓ **Say it Out Loud**

✓ **Do it Now**

You've heard me say this before. **Write it down.** Remember Artie, the introvert from Chapter 4? He carries a small pad and pen in his pocket and is always ready to jot down an idea or two. Some people have a pen and pad on their night table next to their bed, so when they have an idea in the middle of the night, they can **write it down.** I carry a pad and pen with me most of the time.

If you **say it out loud,** the "it" becomes a reality. Say your idea in front of a mirror, say it to your friends and family, just say it out loud. I find the more I say my idea out loud, the clearer it gets. After I say it out loud, I then have to pull out my trusty pad and write my newly articulated "it."

It might take you an hour or a month to move through the three steps and come up with an idea for a talk. If you feel good about the topic you selected, then do something about it. Contact the workshop or seminar coordinator, write an outline, and beef up your bio. **Do it now.**

More work for me

The toughest part about presenting a talk is not actually presenting the talk, it's writing the proposal (if requested). Every time I look over a proposal to present a paper or conduct a workshop at a conference, I cringe. Take your time writing it and ask the conference coordinator for help, if you need it.

Here's what I recently had to do prior to participating as a speaker in a one-hour teleseminar.

1. Write a one paragraph biography
2. Write two learning objectives
3. Attach a head shot photo
4. Sign a five-page release and authorization form
5. Write an outline of key talking points for the presentation

Another time, I was asked to give a talk on marketing diagnostic imaging services at a national medical conference. When I received the speaker's information packet, I was taken aback. I was only allowed to use my company's logo one time in my presentation. It had to be on my title slide. I could not make any reference (on the slides and during the talk) to my company and what I did. I had to bite my tongue in order to get through my presentation. A word to the wise: read the fine print.

Don't share your toys

Early in my career, one of my work colleagues said I should never use someone else's slides when making a presentation before a group. I ignored the advice. Several months prior to the time of my scheduled talk, I sat in on a colleague's presentation at a conference. I noticed a great slide that would fit perfectly into my presentation. I asked her if I could use the slide and she agreed. When it came time to prepare my talk, I inserted her slide into my presentation and did not think twice about it. When it came time to show this slide, I found myself stumbling and over-talking. I totally misinterpreted the content and context of the slide, even though I practiced prior to the talk. Be forewarned.

Do-it-Yourself

What about conducting your very own seminar, live or online? What about co-sponsoring your seminar with another business or a referrer? Do you have a topic that would draw a crowd? Will you be able to clearly state this seminar is not a sales pitch? How much would you charge? If you co-sponsor a seminar, what kind of company would compliment your business? Is it worthwhile to offer registration at no charge?

⇄ One study reported emails sent using the word **Free** in the subject line were 10 percent more likely to be opened than those without.

I am ambivalent about which words to use if I do not want to charge a fee. Do I use *Free, At no charge,* or *Complimentary*? No matter which media you choose to use, electronic or traditional, you'll want to think about which one of the three options will appeal to your customers.

But wait, I have more questions for you. Where are you going to conduct this seminar? How many months do you need to plan the event?

Conducting a seminar or workshop is definitely considered a traditional tactic. But, think about how you're going to promote the seminar. You'll want to use a combination of traditional and electronic marketing vehicles.

Have Some Fun – Give Something Back

Sponsoring an event is more like publicity than marketing. Your goal is straight-forward; support the sponsoring organization and get visibility for your business. There are plenty of opportunities to co-sponsor an event with another small business owner. Do you know any charitable organizations, which would be a good place to sponsor or co-sponsor an event?

I have a client who, along with five other businesses, co-sponsors an annual fun run. At the end of the race, my client personally hands out tee shirts with his company's logo printed on the back. All runners get the tee shirt. Sponsorship of the fun run allows my client to advertise on all online and written promotional literature. Think of it as getting free advertising.

Lunch Is on Me

Take a referrer to lunch. Consider how much time the customer or referrer has to meet with you over lunch. Would going out for coffee be an acceptable alternative? How many lunches would you want to schedule a month? Nothing beats face-to-face meetings with customers and referrers. One of your goals should be to ask your customer if there are other referrers or customers you should meet.

When I'm asking someone if they would like to go to lunch, I make it a point to say I'm not going to try to sell them anything. Try leaving one day a week open for business lunches.

Be an Exhibitionist

Exhibit at local trade shows and conferences. What is the cost to exhibit? Do you want a pop-up stand or table-top? How much do you want to spend on graphics and giveaways? Before you sign up, find out any other hidden costs there might be.

I've exhibited at professional meetings and business expos and have paid as little as $75 and as much as $10,000 just to rent the space. The good news is that when you sign up to be an exhibitor, your name will appear on the conference promotional program (printed and online), and on the exhibitor list distributed at the conference.

When you exhibit, you show support for the sponsoring organization and are able to meet customers and prospects. You also get new names for your mailing list.

A Teachable Moment

Do you have any experience teaching? If so, why not teach a credit-free course at a local higher education institute? Can you create a course interesting enough to generate interest from the public? Are there courses already offered you might be interested in teaching? You'll spend much more time than you expected preparing your lectures; I've heard for every one hour of lecturing, your preparation time could take up to three hours. You're not going to get rich teaching any kind of course at a local college, but teaching is another way to reach the public in a non-selling mode.

Phone a Friend

Do you know anyone who enjoys making cold calls? If you're thinking of Jordan Belfort (played by Leonardo DiCaprio) in the movie *The Wolf of Wall Street,* you're right; he loved making cold calls. The goal of a cold call is to get a face-to-face appointment, whether the person you're targeting is a prospective customer or referrer. Write a script using the ideas you generated from your power message and elevator speech. If you're going to make a cold call and the call goes into voice mail, don't leave a message. Call back either the next morning or late afternoon.

A Happy Customer is a Repeat Customer

Your retention strategy should be simple and straightforward: Delight the Vital Few and the Middle Majority. How? Think of some type of non-gimmicky customer retention strategy. Look at what your competition is doing. What ideas can you think of from other businesses or professions? Key point: think *customer retention*, not marketing, even though there is a thin line between the two. Both fit the definition of marketing as the management of strategic relationships. It's okay to blur the lines, as long as you know it. If you feel overwhelmed by the idea of starting a customer retention program, put it on your back burner and let it stew.

Everyone knows REI, the outdoor gear and clothing retailer. Its customer retention program is outstanding. Every time you spend money in its stores, a certain percentage of the sale is credited back to your account. At the end of the year, you get cash to apply to another purchase. It also offers member-only deals and discounts. REI knows how to make customers feel special.

After someone attends any of my marketing workshops, I offer them discounted fees for one-on-one coaching. When someone signs up for coaching, I add this person to my Vital Few list. As one of a select Vital Few, they qualify for further discounts on workshops, master classes, and other marketing services I offer. I occasionally send them special white papers I wrote on various topics.

Tool	Target	Tool	Target
Brochure	B2B & B2C	Appear as an expert on local talk radio and television news shows	B2C
Flyer	B2C	Networking: • Attend networking events • Volunteer at the event • Present talk or be on a panel • Attend meetings, conferences and seminars • Start or join a business networking group • Join local business organizations: CoC, local economic development agency, etc.	B2B & B2C
Yellow Pages display ad	B2C	Present talks at local civic, social, community or religious organizations	B2B
Newspapers and/or magazine advertisement		Conduct a seminar solo or with another business	B2B
Newspaper & magazine coupon/insert	B2C	Co-sponsor an event with another small business owner	B2B & B2C
Thank you notes: • Handwritten • Email • Snail mail	B2B & B2C	Take a referrer to lunch	B2B & B2C
Holiday cards	B2B & B2C	Exhibit at local trade shows and conferences	B2B
Newsletter	B2B & B2C	Teach a credit-free course at a local higher education institute	B2C
Letter to the editor: newspaper or magazine	B2B & B2C	Make cold calls on the phone	B2B
Radio and/or TV ads	B2C	Implement customer retention program	B2B & B2C

Weave Your Tactical Tapestry

It's finally time to take all of the traditional tools and tactics listed above (there are twenty) and pair them with a strategic relationship.

For this part of the exercise, list only customers. Go back and take another look at the traditional tools and tactics. Do the following:

1. List up to three strategic relationships with customers in the left column. Do you have three types? If not, list one or two.

2. For each relationship you listed select up to three traditional tools you think would work to build and maintain a relationship. Take a shot at this.

Name of Strategic Relationship	Suggested Tactics
Customer #1	1. 2. 3.
Customer #2	1. 2. 3.
Customer #3	1. 2. 3.

This time do the same thing but substitute referrer for customer. Go back and take another look at the tools and tactics. Do the following:

1. List up to three strategic relationships with referrers in the left column. Do you have three types? If not, list one or two.

2. For each relationship you listed select up to three traditional tools you think would work to build and maintain a relationship.

Name of Referrer	Suggested Tactics
Referrer #1	1.
	2.
	3.
Referrer #2	1.
	2.
	3.
Referrer #3	1.
	2.
	3.

Pat yourself on the back. Your marketing game plan is coming together.

In the next chapter, you'll go through the same exercise but this time you'll be using electronic marketing tools and tactics.

CHAPTER 10

Tools of the Trade 2: Electronic Marketing Platforms

This is a chapter full of caveats. I will not:

- discuss gaming or non-marketing electronic media platforms,
- show you how to set up and post stuff,
- delve into the nuances of each platform,
- WOW you with amazing facts and figures about social media and social networking,
- use technical language I can't understand,
- make promises and guarantees about the effectiveness of different platforms,
- show you my biases – as best as I can.

What I will do is walk you through a three-step process to get your online presence up and running in a manageable way. You'll learn about ways the changing electronic communication landscape affects how you conduct your business. You'll have fun taking the *Are You a Social Media Luddite?* quiz. You'll go through the same type of exercise you did in the last chapter by identifying those electronic marketing tools you might want to use as part of your overall arsenal of marketing tools and tactics.

Let's put the topic of electronic communication and social media in perspective. Here's the way I see it. Social media vehicles (such as Pinterest and blogging) are designed to reach a wide audience. Social networking platforms (such as Facebook and Twitter) are designed to create personal, one-on-one connections. Some social media and social networking platforms are designed to reach a wide audience as well as having the capability to make one-on-one connections. Electronic communication can be used on a desktop computer, laptop, tablet, or other mobile device.

These interactive electronic tools are veritable newcomers to the world of marketing. Amazon launched its website in 1995. LinkedIn went live in 2003. Facebook was launched in 2004. The first Tweet was sent in 2006. The first iPhone was sold in 2007. Instagram appeared on the social media scene in 2010.

The Changing Face of Electronic Communication

The electronic communication landscape is changing everyday. Social media platforms come and go. Newer social networking platforms gain popularity while older ones fall by the wayside. Remember how MySpace was all the rage? Today, MySpace is yesterday's news. In ten years, you might find a dog-eared copy of *Critical Connections*. You turn to a page which discusses Tumblr and you say to yourself, "What ever happened to Tumblr? I don't even remember what it did!"

LinkedIn and YouTube are two examples that illustrate the changing nature of social media and social networking. When LinkedIn launched in 2003, it was THE place to go for networking and connecting with business colleagues. LinkedIn offered a modest job search function. I'm not going to mention any recent or pending enhancements made by LinkedIn because by the time you read this, there will be even more enhancements and upgrades. Who knows, LinkedIn might morph into something else.

In 2014, LinkedIn launched LinkedIn Job Search. Using a mobile device, LinkedIn Job Search now has the capability to point LinkedIn members to nearby job opportunities. It also scans user profiles and recommends other jobs across the country. It's like a job board on steroids (my words). Yes, the business networking feature on the LinkedIn website is still alive and well. Other features on LinkedIn have changed over its brief life-span, too. In addition to the free services offered by LinkedIn, it sells premium account upgrades. Large employers are forking over bags of money to LinkedIn for access to it's massive database of members.

MeTube or YouTube

According to Tad Friend, writing about YouTube in the *New Yorker* in 2014,

> YouTube was adults with camcorders shooting kids being adorably themselves. It was amateur hour. Nowadays, YouTube is alarmingly professional. It has millions of channels devoted to personalities and products, which are often aggregated into "verticals" containing similar content.

Who would have predicted that a revolution in electronic communication would have such a vast impact on business? Twitter, Pinterest, Instagram, and Facebook, just to name a few have expanded their capabilities. Twitter, besides having the ability to link to other (content) sites, is now a platform to receive breaking news. You can set up your own Twitter business page, too. Pinterest now has a blogging feature. Instagram is now a good place to find recipes. LivingSocial has moved away from a deal-of-the-month platform to a promoter of concerts, festivals, and other events. Small businesses that advertised on LivingSocial now have to look elsewhere to advertise.

> **What's one thing you can do to keep up with the latest development in social media and social networking as it pertains to business?**
> *(Example: Set Google alerts for news about social media.)*
>
> _____
>
> _____
>
> _____

You have to make a conscious decision about how much or how little time this might take.

The Social Media & Social Networking WOW Factor

Recently, I was conducting a marketing workshop for small business owners. When it came time to introduce *Tools of the Trade 1: Traditional Methods,* something happened which surprised me. One of the workshop participants blurted out that he had just heard about a cool, new app. To this day, I cannot recall what the app was or what it did. I don't even remember if the app was related to marketing.

But what I do remember is what happened next. The workshop participants turned their attention and focused their energy on what he was saying about the coolness of the app. I felt the energy in the room shift from the topic at hand, Traditional Tools of the Trade, to what this man was saying. Picking up on his enthusiasm, the participants started asking him questions. I realized I needed to intervene before this escalated into app mayhem. It took me a few minutes to gently shift the participants' focus back to the topic at hand while trying not to offend this man.

After the workshop, I told my wife Gail about what happened. I was flabbergasted at how powerful the WOW factor was regarding social media. It was as if I could hear each workshop participant saying to themself, "WOW, that's cool, I gotta get it." The WOW Factor acted as an anesthesia. They got caught up in the excitement of the new social media app, and any logic or rational thought they had was dulled. They didn't see the social media app for what it really was. They were no longer thinking about their real goal – to promote their businesses, using the right tactics.

I too am a victim of the WOW Factor. A friend of mine told me about a new travel app. He was amazed at how many functions this app offered. I got caught up in his excitement. So, what did I do? I went home and downloaded the app into my smartphone. And, there it sits. I've probably used the app twice in a year and most likely will delete it when I can remember it's on my phone.

When I look back at this incident, all I could think about was how people react to a fad. The dictionary defines a fad as "an intense and widely shared enthusiasm for something, especially one which is short-lived and without basis in the object's qualities; a craze." Maybe I'm exaggerating but you get the point.

Back to the workshop. When it came time to discuss the objectives and the messaging strategy involved in using online and social media, no one mentioned the app.

I was proud of myself for giving this phenomenon a name – the WOW Factor. Let's look at this in a slightly different context. I notice people fuel the WOW factor fire when they hear astounding social media or social networking statistics. I do not want to fuel your fire by assaulting you with a list of amazing social media facts and statistics. Here are a few examples of what I mean (without statistics):

- The number of people around the globe who use social media on a daily basis – **So what?**
- The percent of people who access social media on their mobile device – **How does knowing this help you?**
- The best time of the day to retweet – **Do you have to be punctual?**
- The percentage of people who say the design of a website is their number one criteria for discerning the credibility of the company – **What's the number two criteria?**

Is it necessary for you to know about social media facts and figures? I unequivocally say, "it depends." How are all of these numbers and facts going to help you establish and maintain relationships with customers? If you stumbled over answering these questions, move on and focus on your customers.

More Substance Less WOW

I was consulting with the marketing manager at a small trade association. I was hired to evaluate its existing social media and online marketing strategy and recommend areas for improvement. The marketing manager said social media wasn't producing any results. When I asked what results the association was looking for, she said print publication sales were flat and there was a decrease in revenue from online courses.

Two years ago, the marketing manager caught a nasty case of the WOW Factor from the association's leadership (mostly executive board members). They wanted the association to be on the cutting edge of digital communication. Prior to this time, the association's foray into the digital world was its bare bones website. As a result of the association's need to be on the cutting edge of digital communication, it went full steam ahead into the unknown world of social media. Today the association Tweets, posts videos on YouTube, updates its Facebook business page and sends emails to its members and prospects. They had a goal of producing at least one podcast a month. Podcasting never happened.

The marketing manager lost sight of meeting the needs of the members. Instead, she got caught up in the board's enthusiasm with social media.

In the course of listening to this, I noted the association's marketing efforts shifted from meeting the needs of the membership to "let's jump on the social media bandwagon." What happened to the needs of the members? If their needs are not being satisfied, chances are members will not renew their membership. This is the worst thing an association executive wants to hear.

We needed a plan and we needed it fast. Here's what we came up with.

1. The marketing manager would **conduct an online membership survey.** One goal would be to find out which communication vehicle members prefer when receiving information from the association. The other goal was to identify unmet member needs.

2. The association would **suspend any social media or social networking activities** until the results of the survey were analyzed.

3. Based on the results of the survey, we would **build a social media plan** based on member needs.

Here's what we learned from the survey:

- Members rated "networking" as the single most important benefit they got out of their membership.

- The type of networking the members want is live, face-to-face contact with other members at seminars, conferences, and meetings held on a local, regional, and national level.

- The second most important benefit they expressed is getting up-to-date information on the latest developments in their industry.

- The older members who were surveyed did not show a preference for how the information should be transmitted: written or electronic.

- The newer members, as expected, wanted all communication sent digitally. It was unexpected to find that the older and newer members both agreed that face-to-face networking sessions were vital opportunities for professional growth. This information provided all the grist we needed for our marketing mill.

From Analysis to Action

Based on this information, my recommendations were:

- Reposition its electronic marketing strategy to focus on getting members to attend live events.

- Use email and its online newsletter as the primary communication vehicle, including sending up-to-date information on its industry.
- Keep the website up and use it as a repository of member-related information.
- Suspend all Twitter, YouTube, and Facebook activities.
- Assign the intern the job of producing three content-driven podcasts a year.
- Create a series of local and regional networking events. These events would feature a speaker and leave time for networking activities.
- Increase the frequency of emails as a way to motivate members to attend live events.

Because of implementing the above strategies, attendance at regional events began to increase and the number of requests for printed literature (newsletters, white papers, etc.) decreased. Loads of lessons to be learned, but the main message is "know your customer."

Where Do I Start with Electronic Marketing?

With ever-changing online and digital platforms, you might drive yourself crazy trying to figure out where to start. Be sure to calm the part of your amygdala, which triggers reactivity, when you think of using electronic marketing tools. Take ten deep breaths and don't forget to exhale.

Now you are calm enough to set goals for how you're going to use electronic marketing to build and establish strategic relationships with customers and referrers. No matter what platform you use, you'll want to follow these three steps. Go slowly.

Rome wasn't built in a day, neither was a website.

Step 1: Get Your Feet Wet

Test the water so you can get a feeling for working with a limited number of electronic marketing platforms. Your objective is to establish an initial online presence with customers and referrers. In order to avoid coming down with a case of WOW, I recommend to my new clients to use only **one** online platform. It might be as simple as getting your name listed on a local business directory or your professional association's referral list, if appropriate. You can even list your business on Angie's List. Hold off on using the linking or syncing function on your electronic marketing platform. Remember, one platform at a time.

1. Who is your primary (customer and referrer) strategic relationship (from pages 111 and 113)?

_____

_____

2. What is your electronic marketing goal?

_____

_____

3. What do you want to say to them (power message or elevator speech)?

_____

_____

4. What action do you want them to take?

_____

_____

Take your best guess and choose one and only one electronic marketing platform to use before you jump ahead and look at all of the Electronic Marketing Platforms starting on page 153.

_____

_____

Why did you select this one?

_____

_____

Congratulations, you have avoided drowning in the WOW factor. Good start. Enjoy getting your feet wet. You took another big step toward your ultimate goal – building your personalized marketing plan.

Step 2: Wade into the Shallow End

After a period of time (you determine how long this should be), take the next step: wade into the shallow end. Your goal is to offer information (remember, you are a subject matter expert) on topics that would be of interest to your customers and referrers. You are not selling, you are not pitching, you are not promoting. You are sharing information. Talk briefly about your expertise (it's less about you and more about them) and relevant experience as a way to build your credibility. Talk about topics that pertain to your business. You become the subject matter expert, no matter what business you are in. Now:

1. Start building your business website. What's the biggest challenge you face in building and maintaining your website?

_____

_____

_____

_____

_____

2. Build your Facebook Business page. What's the biggest challenge you face in building and maintaining your Facebook Business page?

_____

_____

_____

_____

_____

3. Join and participate in targeted listserv discussion groups. (A listserv or discussion group is an email-based platform. Listservs allow people of similar interest to share ideas, tips, and support each other. Check out Yahoo Groups and Google Groups). Don't spread yourself thin by joining too many groups. Test the waters and see this is a viable platform for you to build and establish yourself as a subject matter expert.

What's your biggest challenge in joining and participating in listservs?

_____

_____

_____

_____

Find some listservs or discussion groups on Google and Yahoo Groups which are appropriate to your business or profession. Identify only one to join and participate in.

_____

_____

↩

If you get stuck, go back to your strengths and challenges in Chapter 2, and remind yourself of your strengths.

Are you getting cold feet after reading the above? No problem. Take a step back. Jettison any thoughts you have about needing to know all about Keywords, Meta Tags, Search Engine Optimization, RSS Feed, etc. While you're taking a step back, feel free to look up these words on Wikipedia

Step 3: Dive into the Deep End

You set the stage for Step 3 by moving thoughtfully through Steps 1 and 2. You have your online presence. You might not be finished with your website or your website might be good-enough-for-now, but that's okay.

You now have the confidence to dive into the world of electronic marketing. So, let's talk about social media/social networking. I prefer to use the term "electronic marketing platform" as a way to include social media and social networking vehicles. I'll use this term as we move forward.

Remember Fatal Marketing Mistake #1: thinking about tactics before thinking about who your customers are and what they need. Chances are each of the strategic relationships you want to build will have slightly different needs and may require electronic communications in a different form.

I know from experience that one of my customer segments – legal professionals – does not use Twitter, does not like Twitter, and does not understand Twitter (my interpretation). I know this segment prefers to receive email from me as a primary means of communication. Good for me, it's one less electronic marketing platform to worry about, in the case of this particular segment.

Now, take a time-out and have some fun.

⤺ ARE YOU A SOCIAL MEDIA LUDDITE?

A Luddite is someone who does not embrace new technology and avoids using it.
Answer each question below, to the best of your ability. Be honest.

1. **InstaGram** is a Western Union product.	Yes	No

2. What is **YouTube**?
    A. Something you plug into a television
    B. A hose on a vacuum cleaner
    C. A Selfie
    D. None of the above

3. A **hashtag** is an illegal drug.	True	False

4. Which of the following device is required to play **Candy Crush Saga**?
    A. Cell phone, computer or tablet
    B. Walkie-talkie
    C. Two tin cans attached with a string
    D. Rotary dial telephone
    E. None of the above

5. A **selfie** is an instance of visceral narcissism.	Yes	No

6. Who founded **FaceBook**? Select only one:
    A. Mark Twain
    B. Mark Zuckerberg
    C. Marco Polo
    D. Karl Marx
    E. All of the above

7. Is your computer more than ten years old?	Yes	No
8. Have you updated your profile on **LinkedIn** in the past six months?	Yes	No
9. Can you name four or more social media/social networking platforms in less than 30 seconds without looking in this chapter?	Yes	No
10. Can a **tweet** be sweet?	Yes	No

Correct Answers:

1 No	7	If you answered **Yes**, stop everything and back up your files on an external hard drive. If you answered **No**, do the same thing.
2 D	8	If you answered **Yes**, then join and participate in one new LinkedIn group. If you answered **No**, wait until you have finished reading *Critical Connections*, and revise your profile using parts of your elevator speech and power message.
3 False		
4 A	9	If you answered **Yes**, consider yourself a non-Luddite. If you answered **No**, consider your self a card-carrying Luddite.
5 Yes		
6 B	10	If you answered **Yes**, continue Tweeting. If you answered **No**, to go Wikipedia and see if you can find the correct answer.

Let's Get Specific

Throughout this book I've been mentioning some electronic communication tools of the trade which you can use to promote your business. Moving forward, I'll be listing only those platforms that relate to directly marketing your business. I've excluded those fun-and-games platforms and any platform that generates revenue from display advertisements. I can't emphasize enough that platforms are changing so fast, it's impossible to keep up-to-date with their capabilities.

In Chapter 9, you identified traditional marketing tools and tactics and have paired tactics with strategic relationships with the goal of building a strategic relationship. Now let's get specific.

- A list of electronic marketing platforms appear in the table that begins on page 153. In the far left column there are seven brand name platforms (this is not an exhaustive list). Nine generic platforms, such as blogs and email, appear on pages 154 and 155.

- The next column, *Purpose,* summarizes the purpose and goal of each platform as it relates to the management of strategic relationships.

- The third column from the left, *How to use it,* suggests some general ways to use the platform in the service of managing strategic relationships.

- The far right column, *Consider this . . .,* offers food for thought about each platform.

Just as you did in the last chapter, look over all of these tactics and then do the exercise that begins on page 155.

⇆ DIGITAL MARKETING TOOLS AT-A-GLANCE

Brand Name Platform	Purpose	How to use it	Consider this . . .
Facebook Business Page	Establish and maintain personal connections Possibly reach a wide audience	Share content Sell a product or service Post a quote Pass on articles of interest	Functions are updated and sometimes deleted. Not generally used to broadcast information to the general public. You have to be committed to posting content daily or weekly. Occasional posting doesn't build connection or a wider audience.
Twitter	Establish and maintain personal connections Possibly reach a wide audience	Link to websites or other content platforms to increase traffic Find other people and/or businesses with the same interest Promote a product or service	How much information can you communicate in 140 characters? You have to be committed to tweet daily or weekly. Occasional posting is not an effective way to increase the number of people who follow you.
Instagram	Establish and maintain connection with customers	Send visuals (video/photo) and short messages to your target audience using a mobile device	Keep customers continually engaged by having a personal experience with your product or service. Examples: • Promote a photo contest • Offer discounts • Share customer experiences • Motivate them to attend an event
Tumblr	Engage a wide audience	Share creative visuals (artwork, animation, photos), inspirational messages and information	Can creatively connect with Millennials. If someone shares your Tumblr link, it will go back to your Tumblr message, giving you more traffic.
Pinterest	Engage a wide audience	Generate, share, gather and repost information in the form of images or video that meets the needs of your customers	You can't share anything without a visual. Collaborating with other Pinners, who have a large following, will increase your visibility.
LinkedIn	Engage a wide audience Create personal connection	Post your profile and resume Join and participate in groups Promote events Share content Link to your other online media	It's a business networking website that includes an extensive job search function. It's your online resume. You can position yourself as a subject matter expert. Post often to enhance your visibility.
Reddit	Engage a wide audience Bring larger communities of similar interests together	Share information through words and visuals Generate discussions Link to other content sites	Promoting your product or service is prohibited. Confusing to use and requires learning the system and etiquette. Requires ongoing activity of a substantive nature to be worthwhile.

Generic Platform	Purpose	How to use it	Consider this . . .
Podcasts, online videos, YouTube for business	Reach a wide audience	Share subject matter	There are online resources to help you with the mechanics of producing and distributing your podcast. Your podcast is not about you, it's about satisfying your customers needs. Podcasts are not commercials. Requires consistent promotion using your website and other media. Keep the length of your podcast under 20 minutes. YouTube videos for business are all about subject matter, not sales.
Blog	Establish credibility Build customer loyalty Reach a wide audience	Share subject matter	Requires consistent promotion using your website and other media. Keep your blog short, interesting and succinct.
Email • Constant Contact • Emma • Mail Chimp • Sales Force	Establish and maintain personal connections	Share topics of interest Promote products and service Offer practical tips	Think of using email along with other electronic media to build awareness and motivate customers to purchase your product or service. Avoid **Fatal Marketing Mistake #3** (Chapter 7).
E-commerce aggregate websites • eBay • Etsy • Amazon	Engage a wide audience	Sell your products	Chances are that you'll be competing with other sellers who have the same or similar products.
E-commerce individual business websites (virtual storefronts)	Establish and maintain strategic relationships	Sell products Sell personal and professional services	Make sure your e-commerce site is easy to navigate, has quality photos and sends a clear message. Remember, websites are passive, they work best when used with aggressive electronic media.
Mobile payment aggregate systems • Google Wallet • ApplePay • PayPal	Simplify the payment process	Collect payments	Customers perceive mobile payments as easy-to-use and more secure.

Generic Platform	Purpose	How to use it	Consider this …
Customer loyalty program aggregators • Belly • Foursquare • FiveStars	Establish and maintain relationships with customers on a one-to-one basis	Sell products by offering discounts or free products to returning customers	Some brands have their own loyalty programs. Your job is to get listed by one of the loyalty program aggregators.
Daily deal websites • Groupon • LivingSocial • GoldStar	Reach a wider local audience	Promote products, services and events by selling at a discount	They charge a commission. Can generate more demand for your product or service. Can increase word-of-mouth interest.
Consumer review sites • Yelp • Trip Advisor • Angie's List	Reach a wide audience	List your business	Listing your business expands your audience. The disadvantage is that you cannot control reviews or hide a post. Be proactive and list your business to be sure your business information is correct.

1. List one or two types of strategic relationships with **customers** in the left column.

2. For each relationship, select one or two electronic marketing tools you think would work to build and maintain a relationship.

Name of Strategic Relationship	Suggested Electronic Communication Tool
Customer #1	1. 2.
Customer #2	1. 2.

1. List one or two types of strategic relationships with **referrers** in the left column

2. For each relationship, select one or two electronic marketing tools you think would work to build and maintain a relationship.

Name of Strategic Relationship	Suggested Electronic Communication Tool
Referrer #1	1. 2.
Referrer #2	1. 2.

A Few Words About Email

When you put together a plan to promote your business, it's easy to lose sight of the power of our old friend, email. According to a study conducted by McKinsey & Company, in 2013:

Why marketers should keep sending you emails —

Email remains a significantly better way to acquire customers than social media – nearly 40 times that of Facebook and Twitter combined. That's because of 90 percent of all US consumers still use email daily, and the rate at which emails prompt purchases is not only estimated to be at least three times that of social media, but the average order value is approximately 17 percent higher.

To me, the above quote says it all, but no discussion of email would be complete without mentioning the latest trend – content marketing.

Content-Driven Marketing

My wife Gail, the psychotherapist, and I conduct marketing workshops for mental health professionals who want to build or transform their private practices.

In the beginning, we promoted the workshops by using traditional tactics: snail mail, space advertisements in professional publications, and brochures distributed at local mental health conferences. I used only one electronic platform: email. I took a tried and true copy approach and wrote benefit-oriented promotional copy. Besides giving an overview of the workshops, I'd write things like:

You'll:
- *Learn four innovative methods to expand your practice*
- *Learn how to effectively communicate with referrers*
- *Craft your personalized marketing plan*

These three bullet points represent the epitome of benefit-oriented promotional copywriting. Promotional copy has its place in promoting your business. But now, you'll see how we did a 180-degree turn in our approach. We went from writing benefit-oriented promotional copy to writing content-driven copy.

Gail and I discussed whether we have time to write content-driven emails to our list of prospects as a way to promote the workshops. Researching and writing content-driven emails is time consuming and hard to do. We knew content-driven emails alone would not be effective. We had to make our best guess to determine what additional electronic marketing platform(s) to use. Our message had to stick with our customers. Could we do it? We have jobs, we have a social life, and we are not workaholics.

Side note: There are very few written resources on marketing psychotherapy. I could not find any "content experts." Since I could not rely on quoting or interviewing someone for my content-driven posts, I interviewed myself.

I volunteered to do the heavy lifting on this project. I sent regularly scheduled content-driven emails to our prospect list of mental health professionals who lived within a fifty-mile radius. Gail participated in four listservs for mental health professionals, as a way to spray content to this group of potential customers. Blogging was an attractive platform for us, but it was going to take too much time. In addition, Gail started posting our content on her business Facebook page.

Here's what I did to start.

1. I read my notes from each topic presented at the workshop – there were nine.

2. I wrote as many bulleted points as I could from each topic.

3. I took the bulleted points from one topic and wrote at least four content-driven posts. I limited myself to bewteen 100 and 350 words.

4. I wrote thirty-six content-driven posts.

5. Based on my work commitments, I decided to email one post every other week to my prospect list.

6. Gail came up with two strategies to use for the listservs. First, she would respond to posts that discussed marriage and couples counseling or posts that asked questions about practice management or marketing. Second, she would post announcements about our upcoming workshops.

Here's a content-driven email sent to my prospects:

Lately, there have been questions about the best way to have a web presence for your practice. Building and maintaining your online presence can be a daunting task. If you don't know where to start, consider getting yourself listed on the *Psychology Today* website. *Psychology Today* listings always appear on the first page of a Google search. This provides high visibility for clients seeking a therapist. Therapists have told me they were able to get their listing free of charge for six months, but you have to call *Psychology Today* directly for this. Remember when you write your profile, you are talking to potential clients. Be warm and make sure you explain (without using professional jargon) how you can help them. This is not an endorsement of *Psychology Today*.

Find out more about building or growing your private practice by attending:

Build an Action Plan to Create or Transform Your Private Practice
*Workshops for psychotherapists new to private practice
and experienced in practice.*

As expected, workshop registration increased and I got more business for my coaching practice. It takes plenty of work to push these emails and posts and it never stops.

In addition to writing your own content, there are other ways to communicate content that addresses customer needs. You are the expert and you want your customers to know it.

1. Write "happy ending stories" as they relate to your customers.

2. List tips and how-to suggestions.

3. Cite excerpts from white papers and research studies.

4. Review relevant books or articles.

5. Interview a customer or another expert in your industry or profession.

6. Post a relevant and short video (not more than three minutes).

7. Post reviews and links to interesting articles.

8. Post photos that relate to your industry or profession.

If you want to write a blog, which I don't recommend while you're "getting your feet wet," it's a great platform to communicate your content. You can link your blog to other platforms, too, such as your website, or Facebook business page. Find out where your customers "hang out" online and push your posts to them, if possible. There are useful resources and how-to-do-it tips on content marketing at www.contentmarketingassociation.com and other places online.

Now that I've given you some real-life examples of content-driven marketing, let's hear from someone else.

Content marketing is the means by which you provide substance to your target group which they can utilize. When executed effectively, you will gain brand awareness, customer acquisition, lead generation and customer retention.
—The Social Media Way of Life for B2B Experts and Content Marketers, 2012

It looks like I've scored a home run. Gail and I positioned ourselves as experts. We increased workshop registration. We added more names to our lists and my consulting business grew as a result of increased workshop attendance.

⚡
Content-driven marketing is building strategic relationships without selling.

What's All the Fuss About Brands and Branding?

The year is 1975. A consumer, Nancy G. walks into a department store (it could be Sears, JCPenny or Macy's) looking to buy a refrigerator. She finds the major appliances section and starts perusing the merchandise. She is confronted with all sorts of choices; color, size, and price. A salesman approaches her and asks if he can help. "There are so many types of refrigerators to choose from. I purposely came to this store because I know your prices are good," she said. Then she asks, "Which one would you recommend?" The salesman points out two models. He talks about the high quality of manufacturing that went into making one refrigerator a top seller. The price of both refrigerators is the same. She picks a color and buys the refrigerator. While paying the cashier, she says, "I can always trust the quality of the brands here."

Fast forward to today. Nancy (with some gray hair) needs a new refrigerator. After all, the refrigerator she has is 40+ years old. So what does she do? She asks her Millennial daughter, Kayla, for help. The first thing Kayla does is ask her mother what features she is looking for in a refrigerator. In 1975, it was nearly impossible to get information about the features of the refrigerator prior to going to the store. Consumers relied on the perceived quality and reputation of the brand. Back then consumers were loyal to brands.

The second thing Kayla does is go online and search, "What questions to ask before buying a refrigerator." She finds several websites with this information. Kayla discusses the questions with her mother and comes up with a list of features her mother wants.

The third thing Kayla does is browse websites such as Amazon, Best Buy, CNET, Walmart, and Sears. She is looking for:

- all the features her mother wants,

- the right price,

- consumer ratings of four stars or more, and

- relevant information gleaned from customer reviews.

Now Kayla has tons of information to help her mother make an informed decision. The mother and daughter team is ready to spring into action. They go to the store. The salesman approaches them and discusses the features and models they are considering. The salesman tells them there is a different model, which just went on sale today. This is not one of the refrigerators they had selected. The salesman tells them it was just like the one they wanted. Something's wrong. The price is hundreds of dollars less than the other model.

What does Kayla do? She whips out her smartphone, gets online, and starts searching for information about the other model. Kayla is surprised to read this model will be discontinued. She finds customers complaining about the refrigerator's inability to distribute cold air evenly and that the icemaker is noisy. "That settles it," says Nancy. She will buy one of the refrigerators they selected after Kayla's online search.

That's not the end of the story. At the store, Kayla adds up all of the hidden charges involved in purchasing the refrigerator: the actual price of the refrigerator; the fee to remove the old refrigerator; the cost to install a copper wire water line (a new municipal regulation); the delivery fee and local and state taxes. Kayla knows that well-known and reputable online retailers sell the exact same refrigerator at a lower price, minus some of the hidden charges.

While still in the store, Kayla finds an online retailer who has exactly what her mother wants. It's your turn to guess what the mother/daughter team did? This is a multiple-choice question. Circle your answer.

Nancy and Kayla:
   A. Did nothing and went home.
   B. Bought the refrigerator at the store.
   C. Left the store and bought the refrigerator online.
   D. Bought the refrigerator at another store.

Let's stop here for a minute. Did you notice there was never a discussion of which brand to purchase? Did you notice Kayla relied on customer feedback rather than on the promotional literature supplied by the refrigerator's manufacturer?

Customer Reviews

As you can see, online customer reviews play a major role in branding yourself or your product. Chances are your business will be listed and rated somewhere online. And there's a possibility you won't be the one who posted it. Here are two things to do when it comes to customer reviews.

1. **Encourage your customers to write a review or rate your service.** I often receive an email from retailers asking me to evaluate the quality of their product or service. However, they implore me to rate them as high as possible. Then I get irritated. It's like someone telling you to tell them you like them. Your job is to make it as easy as possible for a customer to review

your business. Ask them for a review in a way that suggests your desire for constructive feedback.

2. **Monitor what others are saying about you.** If you find a site that reviews your business, and someone gives you a less than stellar review, don't take anything personally. My thinking about reviews and evaluations is based on receiving hundreds of evaluations from past workshop participants. If one person gives me negative feedback, I chalk it up to this person's having a bad day or having unrealistic expectations of what they would get out of my workshop. If two people give me negative feedback, I still attribute the negative feedback to their having a bad day. I call these two reviewers outliers. If I receive three or more negative comments, then it's time for me to critically look at what I'm doing. Maybe they are right. I have to change something. Maybe I need to respond to the reviews in a way that shows customers I take their reviews seriously. Do not minimize the importance of customer reviews.

Branding & Personal Branding

⇆
Most branding strategies are designed for large corporations who are competing for huge chunks of market share. Are you competing for a chunk?

My intent here is to give you a quick look at branding and to stimulate your thinking so you are prepared to venture off and start branding your own business. Entrepreneur.com defines branding as, "the marketing practice of creating a name, symbol or design that identifies and differentiates a product from other products."

What should you know about branding in general without wallowing in the weeds?

• Most of what is written about branding focuses on branding for corporations.

• Most branding strategies focus on product branding.

• A brand is more than a:
  - Name
  - Logo
  - Symbol
  - Motto

My definition of personal branding is "a combination of marketing activities you do to influence how others see you." You influence your customers and referrers by presenting a positive image of yourself. Think of personal branding as a state of mind – in your customer's mind. Personal branding and marketing as the management of strategic relationships are one and the same.

Let's get closer to home. Branding is not about using spin doctors (spokespersons whom you hire to give a favorable impression of you to the public) or publicity agents to manage you as a brand. I'm referring to how you package yourself and project a positive image in the eyes of your customers.

Here's an example of how one woman used a combination of marketing activities (call it branding, if you like) to influence how others see her. Rose is a lobbyist and well-known advocate for low-income housing in her state. She works for a coalition of non-profit organizations involved in addressing low-income housing issues. Representatives of the coalition agreed Rose should be their spokesperson and be the public face of the coalition.

She wanted to build strategic relationships with state legislators and their staffs with the goal of passing legislation to assist low-income families who need affordable housing. In order to achieve her goal, she wanted to be seen as the go-to person in the state for any issue related to low-income housing. She wanted key legislative decision makers to associate her name with low-income housing.

> Personal branding is a combination of marketing activities you do to influence how others see you.

How did Rose initiate the personal branding process? First, she gathered data and wrote a series of white papers based on her own and other's research on low-income housing. Second, she scheduled short, in-person briefings with individual legislators and their staff to discuss key policy issues regarding low-income housing. Third, she started blogging. This was easy because Rose had access to plenty of content from her research.

What's the difference between what Rose did to brand herself and what she did to promote her lobbying services? Nothing. It's the same thing. Don't get trapped into thinking branding is some mystery panacea for your business. Call it what you want; I'll call it managing strategic relationships.

Link & Sync

I couldn't say it better than Albert Costill:

> *Attempting to juggle each and every one of your social media accounts can be tricky, scary and time-consuming. For example, while you're busy updating your Facebook status, you might have forgotten to favorite a tweet. Speaking of tweets, when is the best time to send one out to followers? Ugh. It can seriously give you a migraine.*
>
> *Thankfully, we live in a world and time where developers are rectifying that problem!*

Here's your take-home message regarding linking and syncing. The key is to link your platforms together. Be patient with yourself on this learning curve.

Ready to Move On?

We've covered plenty of ground here. It's time to summarize key points presented in this chapter.

- Social media is changing every day and it's your job to keep up.
- You were warned about the social media and social networking WOW Factor.
- You've moved from analysis into action as you built your marketing plan.
- You used the three-step approach to kick start your electronic marketing campaign.
- You have a handy list of electronic marketing platforms at you disposal.
- Hopefully, you're not a social media Luddite.
- You paired tactics with strategic relationship.
- You learned about branding and the importance of customer reviews.

Coming Attractions

Get ready for a fascinating story in the next chapter. You'll read about the exploits of three young entrepreneurs as they build their businesses. It's the *Tale of Two Clothiers.*

CHAPTER 11

Tale of Two Clothiers

It was the best of times for Beth. And, it was the best of times for Allie and Jenny. Two different retailer clothiers with two different approaches to marketing their business. Both in the start-up phase. Both on their way to becoming successful. Beth, Allie, and Jenny are in their late twenties. Beth is a mother of three and Allie and Jenny are in a long-term relationship with each other. This is the story of their fledgling businesses.

First, a little background about Beth. She and her husband, Adam, lived in a suburb of New York City. When Adam was offered a job in the Washington, D.C. area, they jumped at the opportunity and moved. At that time, Beth was working as a personal shopper at a top New York City department store. Eight years earlier, Beth attended fashion design school. She had the experience and credentials needed to succeed.

"If I don't do it, nobody else will."

When Beth first moved, she looked at the demographic profile of her community and found the population of young couples was growing at a rate above the national average. In her community, there were no clothing stores for women in their 20s and 30s to buy, as Beth put it, "spunky modest clothes." She knew that this group of women cared how they looked. She was referring to Jewish women who want to dress modestly and stylishly.

Beth thought there might be a market for spunky modest clothes for women. So, she instinctively did what any good marketer would. She reached out and asked questions. Beth asked a number of young women what problems they were having in finding spunky modest clothing. She asked what kinds of clothing they would like based on their religious standards. The answers were all the same. There was no place to get this type of clothing. Then she asked a more specific question regarding what type of apparel they couldn't find. The answers were again consistent. They wanted tops, skirts, and dresses. And, they wanted reasonable prices. Beth knew price would be a key factor in determining whether women would purchase her clothes. The women also said the clothes found in department stores and online were not modest enough.

Beth took a deep breath and announced to Adam, "If I don't do it, nobody else will." And that's how Beth started.

"I don't believe this can happen."

That's what Adam said when the first box of clothing arrived on their doorstep. Boy, was he wrong. Beth made the decision to open a "store" based on what she knew, what she heard, and what was missing in the market. Beth found a gap and was going to fill it. Her store would be in the basement of her house. She applied and got a wholesaler business license. She was officially in business.

The first agenda of business for Beth was to attend a fashion trade show in New York City. She knew exactly what types of clothing her customers would buy. She carefully sifted through the merchandise and found just the right modestly spunky clothes. She placed her order for one large box of clothes. Three weeks later, she purchased seven boxes.

Beth's first customer saw Beth's modest Facebook page. Beth does not remember how the customer found her. The customer told Beth she never heard of Beth's store but, "really liked her clothes." When Beth checked her Facebook page, she found most of her friends were from the New York/New Jersey metropolitan area.

Beth knew enough about her customers' shopping behavior that she had to:

- Price her merchandise 40 percent below department stores.

- Accept American Express, in addition to the other major credit cards. Beth knew she would be paying higher processing fees and many stores do not accept American Express. She quickly found out that taking American

Express was satisfying a critical need for her customers: convenience. Beth made sure to tell her customers, "don't leave home without it." This was an important selling point.

- Make it easy to shop by offering convenient hours as well as the ability to schedule a private appointment.

Online Strategy – One Step at a Time

Beth was not in a rush to jump into the world of social media to promote her business. She created a basic business Facebook page. She wanted this as her only online advertising vehicle.

Beth decided to hold off on creating a website. She did not want to spread herself too thin. After all, she wanted a lifestyle that would allow her to spend time with her family as well as run a business. To be on the safe side she purchased a domain name.

Keeping it Personal

In Beth's community, word-of-mouth about anything was a powerful force in terms of influence. One satisfied customer told her friend, who told her friend, etc. What happened? Her primary source of referrals came via word-of-mouth. Beth did not purposely craft a word-of-mouth marketing strategy. Beth was creating buzz for her store.

After being in business for six months, Beth was contacted by a group of women who sold jewelry, cosmetics, and other women's items. They banded together to open a pop-up shop. The location, for this one-day event, which drew more than 100 women was held in one woman's house. Beth considered this opportunity a success for her. As an added benefit, Beth was able to get the names and email addresses of all of the women who visited the shop.

Pop-up shops are temporary retail spaces. Open for one day or several weeks, they range from selling a single product to hosting a private event. On a bigger scale, think of those stores selling Halloween stuff, which pop up in early October and disappear a few days after Halloween. This particular group of retailers set-up a one night pop-up shop. The organizer of the event took responsibility to promote the event. Beth sold all of her clothes and took orders for more. This was a total marketing success.

Soon after the pop-up event, Beth decided to expand her marketing efforts. She rented a booth at a local fund raising event. She was the only retailer selling spunky stylish clothes. Once again, she was able to sell clothes and expand her reach into the local and surrounding communities.

Beth has taken the concept of providing excellent customer service to a new level. From a marketing perspective, she is building and maintaining relationships. She prides herself on her personal approach to her customers' needs. She invites customers to her house to try on clothes. She makes every effort for her customers to feel special. Beth constantly exceeds her customers' expectations. She goes to great lengths to sell eye-catching wrappings. She's open late in order for her customers to shop after work. Customers can make appointments. Beth has a no-strings attached return policy. According to Beth, this liberal return policy is unheard of in her community.

During the holiday season, Beth sent boxes of chocolate with thank you notes to her top ten customers. This customer appreciation gesture goes a long way in building and maintaining relationships.

Beth decided to do something special for her customers and prospective customers. She set up a backyard event in the early evening at her house. At the event, Beth provided refreshments and soft drinks. She assigned Adam the job of starting and maintaining a fire pit. And, of course, she displayed her latest styles. She sold plenty of clothes that evening. Besides telling her customers, Beth only used her Facebook page to promote the event.

I advised Beth to keep a database of her customers and prospects. Building the database can be as simple as creating a spreadsheet and listing the customers' name, street address, city, state, zip, email, items purchased, date of all contacts, and how customer found about Beth's store. I suggested that as her business grows, she might find more categories for her database.

Let's review Beth's journey, so far. She:

- Identified her strategic relationships
- Recognized a need
- Found a way to fill the need
- Slowly rolled out her marketing program

- Set up a reward program for her top-tier customers
- Initially relied on word-of-mouth referrals
- Focused only on Facebook for her online presence.

I asked Beth what her marketing plans were for the near future. She was straightforward and said:

- Build a website
- Open a brick-and-mortar store
- Expand my reach to cover the entire country

When I asked her what her merchandising strategy would be, she unflinchingly said: I want to expand to a one-stop shop selling maternity clothes, shoes, tights, and accessories. I want my customer to walk out of my store with a complete outfit.

Beth took an old-school approach to promoting her clothing business. She did this in part because the demand for her clothes spread like wild fire via word-of-mouth.

The Other Clothier

Allie, my daughter, and Jenny live in New York City. They both have day jobs. Jenny is a marketing manager for an online marketing research company and Allie works as a fashion photographer at a retail clothing chain.

They like to shop for clothes. On the weekends, they would comb department stores, boutiques, and specialty clothing shops looking for the right look. But when it came time to find the right style and the right size, their shopping experience fizzled out. They would leave these stores empty handed and sometimes empty hearted.

"If you want something badly enough, you just have to do it yourself."

One day, while eating brunch in their New York City apartment, Allie blurted out, "We need to work on some kind of creative project." Jenny was taken aback. "But we have good jobs!" Allie then reminded Jenny about how frustrated they got trying to find clothes they like. The clothes they found were too feminine, too masculine, too boring.

Putting on her marketing hat, Jenny said, "Why not, instead of selling menswear which fit into feminine style and visa versa, we offer styles which are slightly adapted to fit women. They came up with the idea of being a retailer of "contemporary fashion for women seeking clothing that blurs the line of modern masculine and feminine style."

After talking to their friends, Allie and Jenny realized they weren't the only ones who were looking for such clothes. Other clothiers were selling this type of clothing but Allie and Jenny wanted their personal touch to be reflected on the clothes they sold.

Crowd Control

In order to get their business up and running, they turned to the internet and used crowdfunding to finance the initial stages of their business. Crowdfunding is a way to obtain small amounts of money from many people. There are hundreds of crowdfunding platforms. Two of the most popular are Indiegogo.com and Kickstarter.com.

According to Forbes.com:

Each (crowdfunding) campaign is set for a goal of an amount of money and a fixed number of days. Once the project is launched, each day will be counted down and the money raised tallied up for visitors to follow its success. Instead of traditional investors, crowdfunding campaigns are funded by the general public.

Allie's and Jenny's goal was to raise $10,000 from their crowdfunding campaign to be used to start building their online store. The campaign yielded $12,500. Perks, offered to those who contributed money, ranged from receiving a limited edition tee shirt for a contribution of $30 to a personalized styling session with Allie and Jenny for a contribution of $400.

Online and On Target

How were Allie and Jenny able to raise that amount of money in 34 days? You guessed it, by using Facebook, Twitter, Tumblr, Instagram, Pinterest, Buzzfeed, and their existing barebones website. I was surprised to hear Jenny say they don't have the resources of time and energy to be involved effectively in every social media platform.

Allie and Jenny's Tumblr page shows photos that range from their line of clothes to personal photos of Allie and Jenny. After one year in business, their Facebook page amassed more than 3,500 Likes. They Tweeted more than 2,600 times. On Instagram, they posted more than 900 times and have 6,400 followers. They pinned more than 520 times on Pinterest. After an article appeared on a Buzzfeed post which was linked to Allie and Jenny's Instagram platform, their Instagram followers doubled in just a few days.

I asked Allie and Jenny why they did not use SnapChat. Allie said they like to control the quality of the pictures that appear in public and they cannot do it on SnapChat. Jenny firmly stated SnapChat is primarily used by teenagers. Teens are not their market.

In terms of generating buzz and capturing email addresses, Pinterest was the least effective platform for them. Allie said Pinterest was a good way for most retailers selling clothing and accessories and those selling household goods to get business. However, they claimed their market is not active on Pinterest, but is active on Instagram and Tumblr.

Allie and Jenny, as sophisticated marketers, understood that online and social media platforms were not the only way to sell clothes. To introduce their online store to their potential customers, they used social media to promote a runway fashion show in a bar in New York City. They attracted customers and got the media attention they were hoping for. During the first year, they were interviewed by six fashion style blogs and five online fashion news e-zines (online magazines).

Up Close and Personal

The runway fashion show was a big hit. In addition, they rented a table at a one-day local street fair and sold enough clothes to cover the cost of the table rental fee. They were not pleased with the idea of selling at a street fair. They realized most of the shoppers were looking for bargains. Their line of clothes was far from bargain priced.

Allie and Jenny were invited to sell their clothes at a night market – an informal bazaar or street market held at night, usually featuring music and boutique vendors. The cost to rent a table to display their merchandise was $175 a night. They decided to display most of their clothing, but only sold accessories. Allie and Jenny knew that since there was no place to try on the clothes, they'd be better off just selling accessories.

They posted the event on Facebook and sent emails to their list of customers and prospects. More than 400 people attended the event. They made a small profit and more important met face-to-face with their target market.

Allie and Jenny are proud of their website. The feedback from friends and customers has been consistent: it's bright; it shows off clothing in a clear way. The use of models helped potential customers see what the clothes look like on a person; and, the photography was creative.

Allie and Jenny have two long-term goals for their business. The first goal is to open a brick and mortar store in New York City. The second goal is to design their own line of clothes and sell them wholesale to retail stores. Good luck, Allie and Jenny!

Lessons Learned from Beth, Allie and Jenny

- Beth, Allie and Jenny had a clear vision of what they wanted before they started doing business.
- They started small and slowly increased their product line.
- They had a clear understanding of the purchasing habits of their respective markets and made the buying process as easy as possible. Remember, a key selling point Beth used was to make sure her customers knew she accepted American Express.
- They are continually looking for and purchasing new styles, which fit their respective markets.
- They knew that in order to keep their eye on the market, they had to communicate regularly with their strategic relationships. Allie and Jenny via social media and Beth via word-of-mouth and personal connections.

As of this writing, it's still the best of times for the two clothiers.

CHAPTER 12

Tactical to Practical

I interviewed three digital marketing professionals: Xande Anderer, a website builder; Kelly Dillon, a social media consultant; and Elizah Epstein, a graphic designer. Think of these interviews as consumer guides. Xande and Kelly will share information which will make your life easy when it comes to building your website and creating a social media program. Elizah will tell you what you need to know before hiring creative professionals.

What You Need to Know About Websites: An Incomplete Guide
Q & A with Xande Anderer

Graphic designer **Xande Anderer** has been fortunate. In the course of his career he's been witness to the twilight of the paste-up era, the rise of desktop publishing, and the birth of web design. He has made his mark as an illustrator, designer, and publications consultant for a wide range of clients in the Washington, D.C. area, and worldwide, most recently as president and creative director at Citizen X Design, xande@citizenxdesign.com.

I sat down with Xande to talk about what you need to know about building and maintaining your website. Why Xande? I wanted to interview someone who brings a graphic design perspective to creating websites and who builds websites every day.

My comments appear in the margin, identified with "EL" at the end. Another caveat: it's easy to get swallowed up in the intricacies of how websites work and get lost in technical jargon. In this case, I think a little knowledge is a dangerous thing. If you focus on the technical details, you miss the strategic issues and lose sight of your website's goals. Let's hear what Xande has to say.

Q. What's the difference between a business website and a personal website?

A. First of all, business websites can be designed either as an e-commerce site or as a professional or personal services website. In the case of an e-commerce website, you require back-end support. These programs are provided by a third party. This includes installing programs which run different parts of your website such as your shopping cart. You also need scripts (small programs which convert data into an email) or little plug-in programs. A plug-in is software which processes content such as Adobe Flash Player. This plug-in enables you to look at a video on web. An e-commerce website needs some form of security software so customers can feel safe when using their credit cards.

Professional and personal services websites generally do not require most of the back-end capabilities needed to run an e-commerce website. Back-end capabilities differ from front-end capabilities. The front-end is what the visitor sees. The server and any other programs I mentioned above live in the back-end.

Professional or personal services websites can take the form of brochureware. Brochureware is an online brochure, of sorts. When you use brochureware, you convert promotional literature (fact sheets, etc.) into web pages. These websites are heavy on content. All they really need is content, a domain name, and a host. You don't need complex computing.

Q. What are some "must haves" on a business website?

A. You'd be surprised at how many business websites do not give the location of their business. Sometimes, I come upon a website and find the copy so vague and the graphics so unnecessary, I can't figure out what the website is all about. This might seem like common sense, but I've seen websites where I have to make a big effort to locate the business's contact information, telephone or email address. Keep in mind the average person will spend just a few seconds on your site. A good designer will work with you to make sure everything you need is included. When you build a website, you have to assume anyone (customers, referrers or web surfers) who stumbles on your site knows nothing about you and what you do. You also assume they don't know your jargon. Visitors need to immediately know what you sell or what services you provide. Example. If you are a plumber, you should show a picture of a wrench and other plumbing tools. If you're selling fine art, then your photographs must have high visual impact.

Q. What are the pros and cons of building a website yourself?

A. Doing it yourself will keep your costs down. You're not paying professionals for design and development fees. You're not paying someone to make changes to your site. You can do it yourself. If you hire someone to make changes, you are going to be beholden to them. When you do it yourself, you can make the changes on the fly. If someone else does it, you might have to wait until they have the time to do it.

If you want to do it yourself, you can use self-publishing web platforms such as WordPress. It is free and is "open source" software, which means it can be created and modified by anyone, at no charge. WordPress originally was created to build blogging websites. Today, web designers are using open source software. One benefit to you is the designer can create the website and you have the capability to change it.

One of the drawbacks of using open source software is the lack of creative choices you have. Most templates are fixed, which means graphics are in a fixed place with a fixed size and tabs have to go in some other fixed place. So, most of these websites look alike.

Q. What are the costs involved in designing and maintaining a website?

A. If you want a professional to design your website, your biggest cost would be in hiring a professional graphic designer. A designer might charge you a flat fee for the entire project based on, for example, the number of pages you want. I know some designers who charge by the hour. If you're going to do it yourself and don't want to use open source software, you might pay somewhere upwards of $500 for a design program.

Other costs include purchasing your own domain name. You have to pay a monthly fee to the place which hosts your website – this is the actual location where all your web files are stored. Other costs might include: a professional photographer; a copywriter; the fee for the right to use some artwork. One way to keep your copywriting cost down is for you to write the copy and have a professional copywriter edit what you wrote.

Q. What's the difference between a designer, programmer, and developer?

A. I'm asked this question frequently. Think of the website designer as a building architect. The architect is interested in the visual presentation, the uniformity, how well everything works together. The architect draws a sketch and hands it to the building construction company. Now think of the web programmer and developer as the building construction company. The terms programmers, developers, and database managers are pretty much the same. These are the guys who build the back end – the things you don't see, like coding and script.

However, if you want a simple website with little or no bells and whistles, a good designer can build your back end. In terms of costs, a designer might tell you the programming costs are billed separately.

Look at online portfolios. Which copywriter understands your business? Ask a lot of questions before you hire. –EL

Q. Should I write all of the copy or hire a writer?

A. As I said earlier – you can give it a shot and write all of the copy yourself. You're the expert. You know best how to describe what you do. Or you can hire a writer to write the whole thing, or hand it off to a copywriter to edit.

Q. What are the three biggest mistakes made when designing a website?

A. From a design perspective and without getting too technical, I'd say the legibility of the words – the physical ability to read a page. It is problematic when the type size or color is not appropriate.

Legibility is the ability to distinguish individual letters without effort. *Readability* is how much effort is required to scan text. –EL

The second most common mistake is putting critical content "below the fold" rather than above the fold. You don't want to scroll down the page to get to the important stuff.

Below the fold: a newspaper layout term. The most important content should be visible at the top of a website's front page. –EL

The third most common mistake is what I call "scope creep." I've been in situations where I'm about 90-percent finished with the design of the website and ready to hand it off to the developer. The client calls and wants me to add more pages to the site. Even though I have a written agreement with the client, scope creep can also result when the client underestimates how much information is needed in the website.

You asked for three mistakes, but I have to mention a fourth mistake. Some people design their website and insert links which take the visitor out of their website and into someone else's website. You don't want to encourage people to leave your site.

Q. What technical terms do I really need to know?

A. You should be aware of the term Search Engine Optimization (SEO).

SEO is the process of increasing the number of visitors to a website by making sure the site appears high on the list of results returned by a search engine. –EL

You should know the difference between a domain and hosting. The domain is simply the name of your website. Hosting is where your files are stored.

Bandwidth is the amount of data which can be transferred to your computer from another website or from an internet service in a fixed amount of time. Bandwidth is different from storage. Storage, in computer language, is simply the amount of space your website files take up.

Another set of words which get confused is hit vs. unique visits. A hit occurs anytime a visitor clicks on anything on your website, such as a file or graphic. Unique visitor refers to how many different people request pages from the website during a given period, regardless of how often they visit. Visits refer to how many times a site is visited, no matter how many different visitors there are. Counting unique visits is a more accurate way of measuring activity on your site.

Q. How much does hosting cost?

A. Typically, you will pay a one-time price for the website and a monthly price for hosting. The hosting price can vary from a very small "hosting only" fee to fees which include updates for your site. Make sure you understand exactly what you will be charged every month by this web hosting company. Prices go from $5 a month up to $100 a month depending what additional services you want.

Q. How much do updates cost once a website is launched?

A. Websites are not billboards. You don't launch them and forget about them. Technically, a good website is always under construction. Your website should change every month in order to keep it fresh and relevant. Ask your web developer how much updates cost. If they charge an hourly rate, ask if it is in one-hour minimums or if is it broken into 15- or 30-minute increments. Some web developers will include a certain amount of updates in the total cost. Ask your designer if you have the ability to make changes. If so, you'll save time and money.

Social Media: Q & A with Kelly Dillon of NakedGirlMedia

Kelly Dillon is founder and director of NakedGirlMedia, born out of the success of her award-winning lifestyle blog *Naked Girl in a Dress.* Kelly and her team run a full-service digital media agency working to help clients with web design and development, social media, email marketing, digital advertising, blog writing and training.

Here's what she has to say about using social media for business. My comments appear in the margin, identified with "EL" at the end.

Q. How is using social media going to help me?

A. If done right, social media will help a business owner build brand recognition; create a network with referrers and customers and increase sales. For small businesses, using the right social media platform can help in recruiting and retaining employees. Brand recognition will happen when you put yourself out there and interact with others on those platforms. Think of using social media as going to a networking event. It's an effective way to present yourself in a positive and strong light. You'll build and grow your universe of followers.

For example, a wedding photographer relies heavily on creating and maintaining an extensive network of referral sources. The photographer needs to connect with wedding venues, caterers, event planners, florists, etc. By using social media, these referral sources will learn about the photographer in a much more personal way than by checking the photographer out on his or her website. Hopefully the photographer can meet these referral sources in person.

Job seekers use social media as one way to evaluate a prospective employer. Among other factors, younger job seekers look for vibrant work environments. There's little or no way to determine this by reading job announcements or by looking at the employer's website. Different social media platforms should be used for different goals. Some businesses use social media as one of their recruitment tools. LinkedIn is a good example. LinkedIn places job announcements on their websites. Prospective employees can contact other LinkedIn members and ask for personal information about a prospective employer.

For example, today, Twitter can be used for industry-specific networking. Employees will look for Twitter or Facebook job postings. Some employers use blogs to post jobs; these social media platforms are cost-effective ways to recruit, increase the employer's visibility, and network with referrers.

The downside to using social media for any business purpose is someone might post negative comments about you and your business. There is information online about social media reputation management.

Q. How do I determine my social media goals?

A. First of all, look at goals you've set for yourself for other aspects of your marketing plan. Tie these goals into your social media goals. For examples: one tangible goal might be to get a certain number of followers. Getting followers could be one way to evaluate how successful you are. The greater number of followers you have will help you reach others goals, such as revenue goals. The more followers you have, the greater your reach. You can track number of customers or sales attributed to social media efforts. Another goal might be creating a solid network of referrers. In order for you to do this, you might need to use more than one social-media platform. For example, you can use email to help grow your referrer list. Email is generally not considered a pure form of social media. The strategy is to touch customers and referrers using different media. Ask those who respond to your email to follow you on Facebook and Twitter. This is called cross-platform marketing. You can write a Facebook post and invite visitors to follow you on Facebook.

I want to repeat this because I think this is the most important thing about using social media and the thing most people don't do. Once, you've created your social media goals, create a social media plan. This should be part of your marketing efforts. Focus on specific goals; create your own social media strategy.

Q. How do I know which social media platforms to use for business, and how do I keep current with the latest changes?

A. This is a tough question to answer. Each industry is so different. You should focus on your business goals, your industry, and how much time and money you want to invest. The two worst things a business owner can do are: be in the wrong place by using the wrong platform and share the wrong content.

Based on your business, I think there are two things you need to do to decide which platform to use.

First, read about the various social media platforms. Since social media capabilities and platforms change so rapidly, you should get the latest information about them. For instance, if you look at the top fifteen social media platforms over the past few years, you'll see there have been significant shifts in popularity and use. Things move quickly. So get a general understanding of what's going on. You can get this information if you search for "top 15 most popular social networking sites."

Next, research what is generally recommended for your industry or specialty. The wedding photographer would most likely spend time pinning on Pinterest. A fine arts photographer might post high-resolution photographs on Google+.

> Your decision to use one platform over another is generally driven by your industry. Or by profession. –EL

It's not a daunting task to find out which social media platform works for you. You can look at your professional association or industry trade group's website and see what they recommend in terms of marketing help.

I can't stress enough how fast things change in the world of social media. If you don't keep up with the changes, you might not meet your business goals. In 2012, Pinterest was not a highly ranked social media platform. Recently, it started rising in popularity. In the past few years, business owners asked if Pinterest was important for their business strategy. Now, for some businesses it's really important. As demonstrated by the wedding photographers. Things evolve rapidly. Look at the top 15 most popular social networking sites today. Look at it next year at the same time and see what's changed. Here is a suggestion: If you want up-to-date information about a specific social media platform, get your information from the internet. Books on social media become obsolete as soon as they are published.

> From Zite's website: "Zite evaluates millions of new stories every day, looking at the type of article, its key attributes and how it is shared across the web. Zite uses this information to match stories to your personal interests and then delivers them automatically to your iPad or iPhone"– EL

Look at www.Zite.com. Zite is easy to use and helps you stay current and keep pace with your platform.

You might want to consider hiring a social media consultant to help you write up a strategy. You then implement the strategy.

Some businesses hire Community Managers to push social media content to customers. In general, community managers are proficient at using social media platforms. However, inexperienced community managers may not have the depth of understanding of strategic marketing objectives or understand how to successfully market a business. Social media is not for fun, "it's not about the app," it's about the market. Social media must be viewed from a business perspective, so you can exploit the space to meet your goals. It's more about the space and less about the platform.

Q. If I had to use only one social media platform, what would you suggest?

A. For any industry, I suggest using Facebook's business pages, not your personal Facebook page. Facebook is by far the most widely used social media platform. Your audience is massive, even if you're targeting a specific geographic location. You can create the size of your target market. Local ads can be directed to your designated market.

Q. Can I plan, set-up, and manage my social media platforms by myself?

A. Yes, its going to require a lot of research. Each platform is unique. If you are not careful and don't use the platform the way it was designed, you might turn off some people. A few years ago the use of hashtags in Facebook were considered annoying. No more. Hashtags are now used for searches. Each platform has its own jargon, and what might be socially acceptable on one might be offensive on another.

> A hashtag is a word or phrase preceded by # – a hash or pound sign – used to identify messages on a specific topic. –EL

Q. How much time will it take to be on social media?

A. As much time as you want to invest. Set a time budget in your social media plan and stick to it. Figure out how much time is too much and how much is too little. How much time will you need weekly to work your social media plan? Are you able to track the time? I believe you have to hold yourself accountable. Why? Spending time on social media can be a "time suck." You can get distracted by getting lost on Facebook. What happens when you have too many social media tabs open? You'll probably see something of interest.

Put it aside for later. Limiting your time (being accountable to yourself), will force you to make an effort to use your time wisely. This is very hard to do.

The biggest problem I see is the lack of consistency in posting. I believe out of sight is out of mind. If you take a break for weeks or months, you'll probably lose some followers. You'll most likely have to go back and repost things in order to build up followers. Put bluntly, you are going to lose traction with your followers.

Hopefully, you have a strategy and a schedule which allows you to post daily; some businesses post several times a day. Some users of social media write many posts and save them for future use. Some people say posting content and getting the results you want – more followers, more interaction or more sales – takes thirty posts a week on Facebook. However, you have to watch out for diminishing returns. Figure out how much is enough for your particular industry. If you have time, how many do you think you can do? But keep in mind, as I said earlier, each industry is different. Know how much is enough by looking at what your competitors are doing.

Q. What are common mistakes made by novice marketers who want to use social media?

A. I think novice marketers make three big mistakes: 1. they post infrequently; 2. they don't treat social media as an online community by not interacting with others in the space; and 3. they post only content about their business.

Your mother is the only person on Facebook who wants to hear just about your business. Find out what other interests your followers have and play to those interests. Define your business audience not only by their business needs but also by their lifestyle interests. Post or repost lifestyle-related content. For example, I know a real estate agent who not only posts information about new houses for sale, but posts such things as: tips about home improvement ideas; announcements of new area restaurants; etc.

Q. How do I measure success with my social media campaign?

A. Like any measurement look back at your social media goals and review what you have achieved and where you fell short.

Working with Creative Professionals – Graphic Designers, Copywriters, and Web Developers: Q & A with Elizah Epstein

I interviewed **Elizah Epstein,** Chief Creative Officer at Epstein Creative for this Q & A. Epstein Creative is a full-service graphic and website design studio that provides a full range of professional creative and marketing services. Elizah and I discussed what you should know before hiring a creative professional to help you promote your business.

Creative professionals include graphic and multi-media designers, copywriters, and web developers who work in a variety of settings. They can be self-employed freelancers. They can work in design studios or marketing communication firms which offer branding, logo development, and web services. Full-service advertising agencies offer marketing research services and the full range of creative services, including advertising placement. Some studios and most advertising agencies employ account managers who act as a liaison between you and the creative team. They manage your project.

My comments appear in the margin, identified with "EL" at the end.

Q. Where can I find creative professionals?

A. One of the best ways to find creative professionals is by word-of-mouth. If you like someone's website, logo or printed promotional literature, get the name of the person or persons who wrote and designed it. If you need design work, and have budget restraints, think about going to a local art school. Graphic design students are always looking for work to use in their portfolio. There are design industry publications which have directories of design professionals. For example, you can browse designer's portfolios at www.comarts.com or go to AIGA.org and look under Find a Designer. AIGA also has local chapters. You can post your job on the Art Directors Club website, adcglobal. org. Another place to look is LinkedIn where there are design groups and advertising copywriters groups and you can search for designers in your area. There are crowd-sourcing websites such as www.eLance.com. You can search for multi-media and graphic designers, writers, and web developers. If you see a website you like and you think it's appropriate for your business, look at the bottom of the home page and you'll see the name of the designer who built the website. You can click on their name and go directly to the designer's website.

Q. Should I hire my brother-in-law's cousin to design my website and logo?

My client, a home inspector, wanted help building a website. He had a cousin who designed websites. When I looked at the cousin's portfolio, all of his websites were built for e-commerce transactions – automotive parts, specialty foods, and custom furniture. This was not a good fit.
—EL

A. It depends. If this relative has experience creating websites and logos in your specific industry or business, interview him. Can you have a frank discussion about fees?

Q. What do creative professionals charge for their services?

A. This is a big topic for freelancers and design firms. Creative costs should be considered part of your business start-up costs such as branding and logo development. Creative fees vary by the experience of the designer and location. A designer in Oklahoma City will charge less than one in Chicago. Logo designers charge anywhere from $300 to $8,000. You can look at www.howdesign.com to find hourly rates of freelancers. You are paying for the value, experience, and education of your creative team. Most designers charge by the hour. Some do value-based pricing. Value-based pricing sets the fee for the project based on the value to the customer rather than on the cost of the project. However, most creative professionals charge by the hour. When selecting a web designer, you should find out what the charges are for: your domain name; web hosting; website design and development. If you are not going to handle maintenance such as updating your site or adding blog postings, it would be fine to use these services. To find specific prices go to GoDaddy, Bluehost, or TempleMedia.

Q. Do I need a written contract?

A. Unequivocally *yes*. A written contract protects you and your creative professional from any misunderstanding. A good contract should include: a detailed description of the scope of work, the number of revisions, a delineation of the exact deliverables, wording about the assignment of your logo to you, and a timeline for deliverables. The contract should state the hourly fee and other possible costs such as photography, web development costs, etc., and payment terms. If you want to see sample contracts and Work Agreements, search the web. I've seen one-page contracts and I've seen 10-page contracts.

Q. What do you think of a graphic designer who also writes copy?

A. Look at the designer's portfolio and see if what they wrote is compelling. Ask the designer what they like to do best, write, or design.

Q. Should I work with a freelancer, a design firm, or advertising agency?

A. This depends on the scope of your project and your budget. Generally speaking, freelancers work alone and not with a team. Graphic designers can refer you to freelance copywriters and web developers. A full service firm can meet most of your design needs but using one will cost more than freelancers.

Q. Should I build my own website?

A. There are do-it-yourself website building software programs such as WordPress. The question you have to answer: "Is building my website the best use of my time?" Even though the technology is easy to use, you might get caught in tweaking and tweaking the site. You might consider hiring a web developer to build just a basic layout and navigation tabs.

> The more time you spend fine-tuning your website, the less time you have to go out and build strategic relationships. –EL

CHAPTER 13

Putting It All Together

In preparing for battle, I have always found that plans are useless, but planning is indispensable.
—Dwight D. Eisenhower

Not all tools and tactics are created equal.
—Evan Leepson, 2001

Now that you have identified most of the tools and tactics you need to build and maintain strategic relationships, it's time to figure out how to prioritize them so you can kick start your relationship marketing campaign. You might think this will be a daunting task. It's not. There's a right way and a wrong way to go about it.

The wrong way: After you have gone through all of the exercises in *Critical Connections*, you unsystematically and randomly implement them. In business terms, this is referred to as the shotgun approach to marketing. A shotgun uses cartridges (shells) filled with little metal pellets. As the shell fires, the pellets spread out to cover a wide range. The farther away the target, the less likely the pellet will have any effect or impact. Think of a shotgun approach as a way to cover as much territory as possible with the least amount of focus, the most random way. The shotgun school of marketing embraces the dictum of "more is better."

The right way: The opposite of the shotgun approach is the rifle shot approach. Businessdictionary.com defines the rifle shot approach as a *"marketing strategy in which (in contrast to shotgun approach) the aim is to concentrate efforts on a narrowly defined area or subject in order to achieve a clearly defined objective."*

The rifle shot school of marketing embraces the dictum of "less is more." If you agree using a rifle rather than a shotgun is the right way, then read on.

How Do You Shoot a Rifle so You Hit the Target?

Your weapon of choice will be an innovative method called the payoff matrix. Think of the payoff matrix as a decision analysis tool. The more information you have, the easier it will be to make an informed decision. The payoff matrix makes it easy for you to evaluate, organize, and prioritize your marketing efforts. It makes you think about how you can effectively and efficiently deploy your marketing resources.

The matrix is used to predict how much value (payoff) you will get for the effort you will make to implement a tactic. In other words, "how much bang will you get for your buck?" You will be evaluating each tactic based on two measures: **effort and payoff**.

Using a payoff matrix:

- Forces you to concentrate and focus your efforts on one strategic relationship at a time. You'll be creating a different payoff matrix for each group of strategic relationships.

- Helps organize your ideas. If you get stuck trying to organize your ideas, remember what you learned earlier: Write it Down, Say It Out Loud, and Do It.

- Helps you to consider how much time, energy, and money you might expend.

- Takes the anxiety out of determining where and how to start your marketing efforts.

- Prevents you from getting overwhelmed, distracted or overly concerned with the details or minutia of the tools and tactics you selected. By using the payoff matrix, you can focus on the bigger picture, and answer the question: "**How much value will I get for my money, time, and energy?**"

Here's a conundrum. As a new business owner, you might have plenty of **time** and **energy** to devote to building your business, but have a limited amount of

money. When your business begins to take off, you might have a lot of energy and money but no time to devote to marketing. I hear this all the time, "I'm finally making money, but now I have no time to promote myself." When you work with the payoff matrix, you'll be able to consider each of these variables before you make a decision about how you want to allocate your resources.

You can use the payoff matrix in two ways. First, use it to plan upcoming marketing activities. I recommend planning your activities six to nine months ahead. These are called prospective payoff matrices. Six to nine months after you've implemented the tasks you've laid out, take a retrospective look at your effort and payoff. What did you learn?

Effort: Hard or Easy?

Let's look specifically at how much effort it's going to take you to implement a task. Effort is defined in terms of how much:

- **Time** it will take to implement the tactic. It took me less than fifteen minutes to call a trusted referrer and set up a lunch meeting. I don't consider the time we spent at lunch as an expenditure of energy. I was just accounting for time it took to make the lunch a reality.

- **Energy** you will expend on implementing the tactic. I sent out a series of emails recently to one of my prospect lists. It took little or no emotional, physical, or mental energy to accomplish this task. I was able to accomplish this without having my limbic system get in an uproar.

- **Money** it will take to implement a specific tactic. Will the effort cost you a lot or a little? You make the determination of what is a lot and what is a little. It costs zero dollars to tweet. Writing, designing, printing, and mailing a four-color brochure could cost thousands of dollars.

Time: Tick Tock

No matter what tool or tactic you want to use to build your business, you'll be expending some amount of time to make it work and see results. Ask yourself, "How much time will it take me to implement this particular tactic?" For example, is getting business cards printed a good use of my time? The answer is probably, yes. It's not going to take a lot of time to create and print business cards. I keep on going back to the business card, as a way to dramatize the message even the smallest task will involve some degree of effort.

It took one of my friends five months to build her website from scratch. She spent countless hours writing and rewriting copy, fiddling around with font selections, selecting colors, and searching for graphics. For her, this was an exciting challenge. She did not think building her website was a time-waster.

What about the idea of creating and implementing a content marketing strategy? Is working on this a good use of my time now? Maybe, maybe not. Creating a content marketing campaign requires time to plan, research, write, edit, post, and respond. (As mentioned in Chapter 10, the more you blast your content, the more effective you'll be. That's a lot of blasting time). Ask yourself, "Do I have enough time to do this now?"

Are You Energy Efficient?

In addition to considering how much time it would take to implement a tactic, you want to ask yourself: Do I have the emotional and mental energy to do this? If so, how much energy will this take? Do I have any energy left over to run other aspects of my business? If you're particularly anxious about building your business, your limbic system might get engaged. We know once your limbic system is engaged you won't have access to your prefrontal cortex (your thinking brain goes offline), and you'll waste a lot of energy trying to get back to business.

Go back to Chapter 2 and look at your strengths. Let's assume one of your strengths is public speaking. You decide you'll list public speaking as a tool to build strategic relationships with one specific group of referrers. In this example, speaking in public does not require a large expenditure of energy. For some people, this would make them terribly anxious, but not for you.

Dollars and Sense

One of my clients developed and sells customized estate planning software packages for lawyers. He thought it would be a good idea to sell his software by exhibiting at a national conference of estate planners. When I asked him if he had the time and energy to do this, he said yes to both. We looked into the costs involved in becoming an exhibitor at the conference. Some of the costs he would incur would be:

- renting space on the exhibit floor,

- producing graphics for his booth,

- purchasing show services (electricity, cleaning, drayage),

- shipping,

- designing and printing promotional literature, and

- travel expenses (air fare, hotel and meals) for four days.

These costs were prohibitive. He abandoned the idea of exhibiting. The story doesn't end here. He didn't want to give up the idea using the conference to promote his software. He decided to register for the conference as an attendee, not an exhibitor. At the conference, he trolled the floor of the exhibit hall and met potential customers. Attending the conference was well worth his time. It required little energy and his costs were reasonable.

One year, I was working on my payoff matrix for the upcoming year. I listed "sending content-driven emails to promote my one-on-one coaching" as **easy to do and result in low payoff.** My strategy was to send emails to past attendees of my marketing workshops (I have different email lists for each service I provide). Besides sharing content, I would offer them a special discount on coaching.

One year after implementing this strategy, I referred back to my payoff matrix to see if I made an accurate prediction of easy effort resulting in low benefit.

I was wrong. It turned out that for every fifty emails I sent to this group, I received one inquiry. Each inquiry turned into a sale (one-on-one coaching). Retrospectively, I should have predicted it was **easy to do and high payoff.** No matter what the payoff, the financial costs were negligible.

My wife Gail and her business partner, Gwen Pearl, are psychotherapists in private practice. One of their specialties is sex therapy. Gail and Gwen have maintained strong relationships with OB-GYN physicians in their community. OB-GYNs are considered a primary referral source for clients.

Gail and Gwen are always interested in finding new ways to enhance their relationships with these physicians. Looking back, Gail and Gwen remembered that sending holiday gifts (fruit or chocolate) to OB-GYNs who referred clients in the past year was hard to do. They had to compile a mailing list of the top referrers (and delete duplicates and bad addresses), enter names and addresses into a database, fax the list to the florist, and pay the florist.

The gift baskets they selected were pricey. Gail and Gwen realized physician offices receive many holiday gift baskets. Their basket was hidden among the other baskets sent by all sorts of vendors. There was nothing to distinguish their gift from others. This was a clear-cut case of high effort and low payoff. The next year, they decided to mail holiday greeting cards to ALL of the OB-GYNs who made referrals. This turned out to be easy to do and had a low payoff. They had little expectations that sending holiday cards would actually result in getting more referrals. Gail and Gwen saw this as another opportunity to get their names out to the OB-GYNs.

Is Your Payoff High or Low?

Payoff is measured in terms of attaining any level of benefit, impact, gain, or success. These are relative terms. What an optimist calls a success, a pessimist calls a failure. I like to divide payoff into two broad categories: tangible payoffs and intangible payoffs (relationship building payoffs). Tangible payoffs are reflected in numbers. How many items did you sell? How many new customers did you acquire? How many contracts did you sign?

A relationship building (intangible) payoff is not about generating revenue but more about building relationships. How many referrers did you take to lunch? How many times did you post something on Facebook? How many names did you add to your current email list? How many events did you attend?

Keep in mind that posting something on an electronic platform probably won't immediately result in generating revenue. However, you know one way to begin a strategic relationship is as simple as interacting with your customers online. After all, aren't we in the business of building relationships?

⇄

The payoff matrix is not static. It's a living and breathing marketing road map, not to be stashed away in an obscure folder on your laptop.

Before we break down the components of a payoff matrix, I'm going to give you an example of how I used a payoff matrix to decide how to promote my consulting services to fitness center owners. I had an idea, which would build my credibility with fitness center owners. I would co-author an article with my client who owns a fitness center. The topic would be on innovative approaches to promoting a fitness center. We would publish the article in a fitness trade publication. I thought writing the article would be easy to do in terms of the expenditure of time, energy, and money. I hoped for a high payoff.

Boy, was I wrong on both counts of time and energy. In terms of effort, my co-author and I had opposite writing styles. He is what I call a linear thinker. He was very logical and focused. He took one step at a time and carefully chose his words. I, on the other hand, was scribbling ideas on sticky notes and "coloring outside the lines." It took us three months of back and forth editing to get the article ready for publication.

I predicted a high payoff. My definition of high payoff in this instance was getting the article published in a magazine, which would be read by thousands of fitness center owners. I'd be able to link my website and other electronic marketing platforms to the article. I hoped those who read my article would be interested in hiring me as a marketing consultant.

I submitted the article to two fitness trade publications and never heard from either one of them. I made two more attempts to contact them, and again, no response. This little adventure cost me plenty of time and energy with no payoff. At least this experience didn't cost me any money.

A Look Inside the Payoff Matrix

The payoff matrix is all about how to efficiently and effectively prioritize and deploy your marketing resources. We've discussed the two criteria used to assess each marketing tool or tactic. The first criterion is how easy or hard it would be to accomplish the task. The second criterion is the estimated payoff involved in implementing the tactic. In Chapters 9 and 10 you identified traditional and electronic marketing tools you thought would work to build strategic relationships with customers and referrers.

Start with one blank payoff matrix sheet for each strategic relationship you identified. Think of your payoff matrix as a worksheet to help organize and prioritize your marketing task. It's best to use a combination of traditional and electronic marketing tools when you fill in the matrix. Each of the four boxes represents different combinations of effort and payoff for a tool or tactic. When you build your payoff matrix, you'll be predicting the effort and payoff for each tactic.

⇆ PAYOFF MATRIX

Name of Strategic Relationship ____________________

EFFORT
EASY TO DO
HARD TO DO
The Candy Store
The Gold Mine
High Payoff
High Payoff
Land of Low Hanging Fruit
Devil's Island
Low Payoff
Low Payoff
EASY TO DO
HARD TO DO
EFFORT

Start with the bottom left quadrant, the **Land of Low Hanging Fruit.** Here is where the fruits of your labor will pay off. You exert little energy and get some payoff. Think of these activities as quick hits. A quick hit means if you implement a tactic you'll derive immediate or short-term benefit. A quick hit tool or tactic can be quickly executed. These accomplishments don't have to be home runs or have a lasting effect. Aiming for quick hits is a satisfying way to get your marketing ball rolling and to feel good about your results. I strongly urge you to implement all the tools and tactics you will list in this box. After all, you're in the **Land of Low Hanging Fruit.**

Wait, don't rush into this. Start by naming one primary strategic relationship you identified in Chapter 8.

Name of strategic relationship _____.

The strategic relationship you identified will be used for all tactics on this payoff matrix.

Before you start filling in the **Land of Low Hanging Fruit** box with marketing ideas, write up to three tools or tactics (at least one traditional and one electronic) which would be easy for you to do and would result in a low payoff for the above-mentioned strategic relationship. If you need any help, please refer back to Chapters 9 and 10.

Tactic #1_____

Tactic #2_____

Tactic #3_____

Did you read through all of the traditional and electronic tools? Are you satisfied the tools you selected will be **easy to do** and have a **low payoff**? Remember, having a low payoff is a good thing, as long as it doesn't cost you too much.

The Candy Store box is conveniently located in the top left quadrant. If you think a tool or tactic is going to give you a high payoff, while being relatively easy to do, write it in the **Candy Store** box. Refer back to my example of sending emails to past workshop participants. It was easy for me to do and I benefited from the activity. And, most importantly, I did it repeatedly. Before you start filling in **The Candy Store** box with marketing ideas, do this:

Write up to three tools or tactics (at least one traditional and one electronic), which would be **easy for you to do** and would result in a **high payoff** for the one strategic relationship you identified above.

Tactic #1_____

Tactic #2_____

Tactic #3_____

Did you read through all of the traditional and electronic tools? Are you satisfied the tools you selected will be **easy to do** and have a **high payoff**?

The Gold Mine, buried in the upper right quadrant, is a place where you have to work hard for a long time to reap the benefits of your labor. It is also a dangerous place. You can run the risk of getting buried alive. Even so, you have the potential for a high payoff, but it's going to take time, money, and energy. There is no gentle way to say this; it might take up to six months to implement and see results (payoff) from the tactic(s) you put in this box. You have to think hard whether you really want to go this risky route. Consider the enormity of the task. At this time, it may not be worthwhile for you to undertake tasks that fall into this box.

Before you start filling in **The Gold Min**e box with marketing ideas, do this:

Write up to three tools or tactics (at least one traditional and one electronic), which would be hard for you to do and would result in a **high payoff** for the one strategic relationship you identified above. Remember you're making your best guess.

Tactic #1 _____

Tactic #2 _____

Tactic #3 _____

Did you read through all of the traditional and electronic tools? Are you satisfied the tools you selected will be **hard to do** and have a **high payoff**?

Devil's Island, the bottom right quadrant, is not a fun place. It was a 19th-century penal colony off the coast of French Guiana. When you're in a tropical penal colony, you have time to waste. The same goes for spending time on marketing activities, which will yield nothing. You don't want to wind up there. You can prevent this from happening. **Leave this box blank.** Why would you want to exert energy, spend time and money knowing your efforts will net nothing or practically nothing? There is no reason to consider placing a tool or tactic in this box. However, in a retrospective payoff matrix, you might want to list a tool or tactic here. For example, my wife Gail put "sending holiday gift baskets" in her retrospective payoff matrix.

You're Getting Closer to the Finish Line

I was working with Kerry, an esthetician – a freelance skin care specialist – interested in expanding her business. We discussed at length all of the ways she had promoted her services in the past. We took a critical look at what promotional tactics worked, and what didn't work. I thought it would be helpful for Kerry to have a visual representation of her marketing efforts, so I sketched a payoff matrix based on what we discussed.

Payoff Matrix Example: Kelly
Self-employed esthetician

	EFFORT	
	EASY TO DO	**HARD TO DO**

High Payoff	**The Candy Store**
	• Thank you notes to clients who make a referral.
	• For facial clients:
	  – thank you notes mailed
	  – thank you phone call
	  – offered discount on another service
		The Gold Mine
		• Website
		• Email via Constant Contact
		• Capabilities brochure
			High Payoff

Low Payoff	**Land of Low Hanging Fruit** • Direct mail discount coupon / special offer to clients • Open house with raffle	**Devil's Island** • Print advertisements in local newspaper or shopper • Radio ads	**Low Payoff**
	EASY TO DO	**HARD TO DO**
	EFFORT	

I was struck by how successful Kerry was at retaining her clients. Yes, the old adage is true: it takes less time, money, and energy to retain a happy customer than it does to acquire a new one. Each and every one of her existing clients would regularly receive some type of incentive to return to Kerry. She never thought her best marketing tactics were her interpersonal skills. Kerry's strengths were relational, not technical. No surprise that she struggled with building her website, sending emails, and writing a capabilities brochure.

If you look at Kerry's retrospective payoff matrix, you'll see she made an uninformed and costly decision about advertising on radio and in the newspaper.

Remember my friend, Deb Shaver, the personal organizer? If I had met with Deb before she started her business, I would have created a payoff matrix with her. Together, we would come up with a list of tactics and place them somewhere in the payoff matrix. This is what it would have looked like (this is not a complete list).

First Payoff Matrix: Deb Shaver, professional organizer

Strategic Relationship: consumers with disposable income in Montgomery County

	EFFORT	
	EASY TO DO	HARD TO DO
High Payoff	**The Candy Store** • Join professional association and volunteer to be on a committee. • Work with a mentor	**The Gold Mine** • Face-to-face meetings with investment banks and investment firms who advise clients who want help tracking their income, expenses, and assets
Low Payoff	**Land of Low Hanging Fruit** • Mail flyer to local churches, synagogues • Auction her services at local charity events	**Devil's Island** • Yellow Pages display ad
	EASY TO DO	HARD TO DO
	EFFORT	

I usually keep **Devil's Island** empty, but for this discussion, I filled it out. More on Deb.

The next payoff matrix would have been created five years down the road, after evaluating what worked and what didn't work.

Retrospective Payoff Matrix: Deb Shaver, professional organizer

Strategic Relationship: consumers with disposable income in Montgomery County

	EFFORT		
	EASY TO DO	**HARD TO DO**	
High Payoff	**The Candy Store** • Yellow Pages display ad • Featured in two articles about professional organizers in two local magazines. (The author found Deb through her membership in a professional association.)	**The Gold Mine** • Face-to-face meetings with investment banks and investment firms who advise clients who want help tracking their income, expenses, and assets	*High Payoff*
Low Payoff	**Land of Low Hanging Fruit** • Attend networking events • Post flyers in local churches, synagogues, and all public bulletin boards	**Devil's Island** • Auction her services at local charity events	*Low Payoff*
	EASY TO DO	**HARD TO DO**	
	EFFORT		

I would have never predicted placing a display advertisement in the Yellow Pages would bring business to Deb. I was confident she would get a big payoff from having face-to-face meetings with investment bank representatives. In the beginning, the auction strategy sounded like a solid idea, but Deb's offering a free one-hour assessment had zero return. You may think participating in an auction would get Deb some visibility, but there were so many other companies auctioning off so many different items (tickets to baseball games, free airline tickets, dinner at local restaurants, etc.) that it wasn't successful.

Show Time

It's time to fill out your very first payoff matrix. Using the payoff matrix below:

1. Write the name of your primary strategic relationship on the top of this payoff matrix.

2. Go first to the **Land of Low Hanging Fruit,** pick one tactic, and write it in the bottom left quadrant.

3. Then, for **The Candy Store,** pick one tactic and write it in the top left quadrant.

4. Next, for **The Gold Mine,** pick one tactic and write it in the top right quadrant.

5. Once you're satisfied with your choices, go back and select a second tactic for each quadrant. If you have any energy left, write a third tactic in each quadrant.

Your Payoff Matrix 1

Name of Strategic Relationship _____

You did it! Well, not quite.

As you can see below, there is another blank payoff matrix. Go through the same exercise as above, but this time use another strategic relationship.

Your Payoff Matrix 2

Name of Strategic Relationship _____

	EFFORT	
	EASY TO DO	HARD TO DO
High Payoff	The Candy Store	The Gold Mine
Low Payoff	Land of Low Hanging Fruit	Devil's Island
	EASY TO DO	HARD TO DO
	EFFORT	

You're Almost Done

Remember the days when you were asked to take minutes at a committee meeting? You wrote furiously so you could accurately capture what each person was saying. You tried your best to summarize what people said and what action items were proposed. And worst of all, you had to type them up in some kind of logical format.

You don't have to do it any more. I've simplified your life so you don't have to wallow through pages of notes to figure out what you have to do to implement a tactic.

The form below is called *The Relationship Action Plan*. It's a shortcut way to capture relevant action items that need to be accomplished. You don't need to make a laundry list of things to do. You don't need to rely on your memory and definitely don't need to rely on anyone else to do it.

Your Relationship Action Plan

*Name of strategic relationship:*_____

For this exercise put only one tool from each box in your Payoff Matrix.

	1 Tool	2 What resources do I need?	3 Whose help do I need?	4 What is my timeline?	5 Why am I doing this?
Land of Low Hanging Fruit					
The Candy Store					
The Gold Mine					

Here's how it works.

1. On the top of *The Relationship Action Plan* write the name of one strategic relationship. You'll be using three Action Plan sheets for each strategic relationship, one for each quadrant. Remember, don't even think of going to Devil's Island.

2. Look at the tools you listed in each quadrant and fill in the names of the tools in the left column. Notice your plan has room for only three tactics. Of course, you can list more, but don't make Fatal Marketing Mistake #2 by spreading yourself too thin.

3. Column 2: **What Resources Do I Need?** Make a list of the resources (technology) you will need in order to implement this tactic. No need to go into detail.

4. Column 3: **Whose Help Do I Need?** Whether you're hiring someone to help you carry out this task or you want to talk over your ideas, list anyone in a position to help.

5. Column 4: **When Will This Task Be Finished?** Give yourself plenty of time to go from idea to implementation. My rule of thumb is to double the original estimate of how long a project or task will take.

6. Column 5: **Why Am I Doing This Task?** This is your acid test. Ask yourself the hard question, "Why am I doing this?" Think back to your goals and vision and see if they are compatible.

You've come one step further in the process of building a practical guide to building and transforming your business.

But wait . . . there's more. At the conclusion of my marketing workshops, I ask participants two poignant questions. Now, I'm going to ask you the same questions.

Question #1: What is one new idea, concept, strategy or tactic you learned after reading *Critical Connections?* _____ .

Question #2: Based on what you learned in *Critical Connections,* name one concrete and practical activity you will do in the next week to build one strategic relationship _____ .

Congratulations. Your marketing plan is complete.

CHAPTER 14

It's a Wrap

Look at what you accomplished on your journey to transforming your business. You met some dynamic and successful people along the way like Deb Shaver, the professional organizer, who has had phenomenal success using traditional tools and tactics to build her business. And Nicole, the math tutor, who initially stumbled through a maze of marketing dead-ends. You followed Artie, the introvert, as he identified creative ways to do business by focusing on his strengths. And, don't forget Allie and Jenny and Beth, the young clothiers, who carved out amazing niches for themselves and are on their way to big-time success. You read my story about how traditional models of marketing were not working for me and having the realization led me to the concept that marketing is really the management of strategic relationships.

You got the ball rolling by looking back from the future and articulating the vision for your business. You took a critical look at your personal strengths and challenges and created ways to overcome your challenges.

Would you have ever thought picking up a book on marketing would show you how your brain functions as it relates to helping you hone your marketing skills?

I asked you to be honest with yourself, face your fears of selling, and face your fears of discussing fees. You saw how easy it is to destroy a business relationship. And what about customer loyalty? You witnessed its demise. You dissected consumer needs so you could create product and services, which satisfy customer needs. We discussed how you could go from Mr. or Ms. Fix-It to Mr. or Ms. Listener using a five-step relationship-building tool.

Don't forget how many practical suggestions you learned such as tips to overcome marketing paralysis, how to write a customized elevator speech and power message, how to overcome the Lookout Syndrome, and how to create a personalized networking plan.

You were asked to use an innovative way to look at marketing as the management of strategic relationships and identify customers and referrers as two distinct types of strategic relationships. You designed a program to care for and feed those customers and others who are in a position to refer business to you. You were challenged to do one thing every day that scares you.

It seemed at every turn of the page, I confronted you with another question. Why did I do this? Because, I know you learned the value of asking questions. Remember what Isidor Rabi's mother said, "Izzy, did you ask a good question today?"

Eventually you wound up at the part of the book where tools and tactics were discussed. The information in these two chapters – traditional and electronic tools – could have taken up thousands and thousands of pages in hundreds of books. It didn't happen. These two chapters were not intended to be a marketing manual for dummies. I wanted to condense what I thought were important strategic issues you should know. I was cognizant of the fact that as soon as I wrote anything about electronic marketing platforms – social media and social networking for business – the information would be out-of-date. That's why I kept it on a high strategic level.

A special note about the social media WOW Factor: Were you convinced it's easy to get caught up in the social media WOW Factor? It's okay to say yes. I too got caught.

In both Tools of the Trade chapters, you paired one strategic relationship with traditional and electronic marketing tactics. Your plan started coming together.

You enjoyed some light moments when you took the *Are You a Social Media Luddite?* quiz. Were you surprised by your answers? Did you struggle with the Jargon Buster exercise? Nobody said this was going to easy.

And, what about the payoff matrix? You now have an amazing and innovative tool to help transform your business. I hope you liked visiting the Land of Low Hanging Fruit, The Candy Store, and The Gold Mine. I'm relieved you did not take a detour to visit Devil's Island. Your final task was to use the Relationship

Marketing Action Plan to help you focus on specific tasks needed to accomplish your goals.

I wanted this book to be a resource guide and workbook you can use for years to come. The concepts won't change but the technology will. My goal was to present as much information as you need to build your business using the least amount of words. I hope this was accomplished.

You're armed and ready to go. I wish you success in your business and remember to "ask a good question."